Hospitable Planet

Faith, Action, and Climate Change

Hospitable Planet

Faith, Action, and Climate Change

STEPHEN A. JUROVICS

Foreword by Matthew Sleeth

Morehouse Publishing
NEW YORK

Morehouse Publishing, 19 East 34th Street, New York, NY 10016

Morehouse Publishing is an imprint of Church Publishing Incorporated.
www.churchpublishing.org

Cover art courtesy of Thinkstock
Cover design by Laurie Klein Westhafer, Bounce Design
Typeset by Rose Design

Library of Congress Cataloging-in-Publication Data

Names: Jurovics, Stephen A., 1936- author. | Sleeth, J. Matthew, 1956– writer
  of foreword.
Title: Hospitable planet : faith, action, and climate change / Stephen A.
  Jurovics ; Foreword by Matthew Sleeth.
Description: New York : Morehouse Publishing, 2016. | Includes
  bibliographical references.
Identifiers: LCCN 2015041255 (print) | LCCN 2015041474 (ebook) | ISBN
  9780819232533 (pbk.) | ISBN 9780819232540 ()
Subjects: LCSH: Human ecology—Religious aspects—Christianity. | Climatic
  changes—Religious aspects—Christianity. | Environmental ethics.
Classification: LCC BT695.5 J865 2016 (print) | LCC BT695.5 (ebook) | DDC
  261.8/8—dc23
LC record available at http://lccn.loc.gov/2015041255

Printed in the United States of America

To Raachel
My wife, my love

Contents

PART III: A CALL TO ACTION—LOCAL LEVEL

Foreword

A dozen years ago, I was a physician, taking care of patients in the emergency room and living the American Dream. I had a successful career, a beautiful home, and all the things that are supposed to make you happy. It wasn't until my mid-forties when I picked up a Bible for the first time that I began to question the "good life" I had been pursuing. Jesus helped me see the world through a new lens, a lens focused less on *me* and more on serving *we* and *Thee*.

Since then, my life has taken many unexpected turns, and now I work full-time on a different kind of healthcare: healing the planet. Along the way, I've helped churches and seminaries across the country put the theology of creation care and Sabbath living into practice. I write books on the subject and have spoken with hundreds of groups across the country about living a slower, simpler, more sustainable life. But most importantly, I try to walk the talk.

When I became a Christian, I started looking for ways to better align my beliefs with my actions. My wife and I decided we did not need to live in a large home that used so much energy, so we sold it and built a house with the same exact footprint as our old garage, getting rid of about half our possessions along the way. Over the course of a couple of years, we completely changed the way we live—cutting back our fossil fuel use by more than two-thirds and our trash production by nine-tenths.

You might think that all these changes made our lives more difficult, but the reverse happened. Living out our theology has made our lives much better. We have fewer "things" to worry about, which allows us to enjoy life more.

So when I learned how Steve Jurovics was combining his engineering experience and faith background to help care for the planet, I was overjoyed. Every time he engages in a project with the biblical stewardship mandate in mind, he is helping to heal God's creation. And by sharing what he has learned about environmentally responsible living, he is helping others care for the planet as well.

The book you have in your hands is a call to action. Part I identifies biblical teachings for earth stewardship and how these principles can motivate people of faith to care for the planet. Part II examines how we can shift from fossil fuels to renewable energy and mitigate climate change. Part III explores how we can make cost-effective reductions in our energy consumption and advocate for change in our communities.

It would be easy to look at all that is being done to harm the planet and feel as if the situation is hopeless. But it is not hopeless. People of faith can and should play an important leadership role in healing our ailing planet. My prayer is that you, too, will join the growing movement of people who love the planet enough to care for it as if it were a rare and beautiful gift of a loving Creator.

—MATTHEW SLEETH, MD
Executive Director of Blessed Earth
Author of *Serving God, Saving the Planet* and
24/6: A Prescription for a Healthier, Happier Life

Acknowledgments

For this book, written late in life, I must acknowledge the innumerable literary and conversational encounters over the years that, though most not consciously retrievable, shaped the perspective of this work. I am clearly grateful, however, to Simmy Klein (may he rest in peace), my friend and mentor during my teens, who first introduced me to the enrichment that can result from biblical study.

Carolyn Toben, Sarah Stein, and Yonat Shimron read early versions of Part I of the book, and I am grateful for their thoughtful comments that influenced later versions.

My thanks as well to Ann Regen Myhre for helping to develop the discussion questions in Part I and to the Rev. Dr. P. Joseph Ward for conversations about James Carroll's *Constantine's Sword* and about Christian-Jewish readings of Scripture.

I deeply appreciate the thoughtful critiques of the author Peggy Payne and the various members of her writers' group during the creation of this work.

To my friend Anthony Weston, I express appreciation for many thoughtful conversations over decades and for his literary and educational efforts encouraging an ethical relationship between humans and the natural world.

I am grateful to many friends who, over the years, expressed interest in, and encouragement for, this project.

I cannot overstate my gratitude to my wife, Raachel, whose love and support, wisdom, humor, and writing skills helped me bring this project to fruition.

—Stephen Jurovics
Raleigh, North Carolina
September 2015

Faith, Action, and Climate Change—an Introduction

"Do not think that I have come to abolish the law or the prophets; I have come not to abolish but to fulfill. For truly I tell you, until heaven and earth pass away, not one letter, not one stroke of a letter, will pass from the law until all is accomplished."

Matt. 5:17–18

"But it is easier for heaven and earth to pass away, than for one stroke of a letter in the law to be dropped."

Luke 16:17

In the Sermon on the Mount, as it appears in the book of Matthew, Jesus said he came to fulfill the Law and the Prophets. The book of Luke expresses a similar adherence to the Law. What in English is translated by Christians as "the Law," Jesus called *Torah* in Hebrew and *Oraita* in Aramaic. Genesis through Deuteronomy, the first five books in the Christian and Hebrew Bibles, comprise the Torah.[1]

Genesis opens with the story of creation, revealing that everything that exists was created by God, and Genesis 1:28 finds God granting the created world to humankind to master and to rule. We are granted dominion over the animals, the fish, and the birds, but the land itself is not mentioned. We would be mistaken to view this as implicitly included, for in Exodus 19:5 God states: "Indeed, the whole earth is Mine."

This verse in Exodus complementing the "dominion" passage in Genesis provides just one example of the need to understand the teachings about God's creation in "the Law" collectively, that is, to draw conclusions from those verses when they are taken together. Each such verse provides its own

---

1. Torah in this instance refers to the part of Jewish Scripture in the books Genesis through Deuteronomy. Jewish Scripture includes thirty-nine books divided into the Torah, the Prophets, and the Writings, and the word "Torah" can refer to all of them or to the entirety of Jewish learning.

instruction within the context of its section and may also clarify a passage appearing elsewhere or significantly alter our understanding of it.

We can take this "collective" idea to its extreme when we ask how to summarize what Christians call the Old Testament. Jesus said: "In everything do to others as you would have them do to you; for this is the law and the prophets." (Matt. 7:12) A contemporary of Jesus, the first-century scholar Hillel said: "What is hateful to you, do not to your neighbour; that is the whole Torah, while the rest is the commentary thereof; go and learn it."[2]

This book seeks first to develop a similar biblical unity, not for all of Genesis through Deuteronomy, but for its teachings about the natural world. When all the environmental-related verses are taken together, what overarching perspective emerges about how we are to interact with God's creation?

This question cries out for an answer as soon as we realize that our use of the natural world can be understood to be abusive and self-destructive. Can we find biblical cover for blasting the tops off mountains to mine for coal,[3] pouring toxins into rivers that then poison fish and corrupt drinking water, for sending toxic fumes into the atmosphere that foul the air we breathe and change the climate? People of faith strive to live in accord with biblical teachings and visit houses of worship to obtain reminders of what our sacred texts ask of us.

We are at a perilous moment in the history of humans on this planet, given the changes in our climate that are underway. The concentration of carbon dioxide (CO_2) in the atmosphere is now at a level not experienced in about three million years, due largely to the burning of fossil fuels. Continuing increases are predicted to bring devastatingly disruptive changes to our world: to humans and non-humans, to the air, to the water, the trees, and the land of this planet. Our descendants will not forgive us if we choose expediency over preserving a hospitable planet.

I believe people of faith can strengthen their connection to God, for I believe it has been weakened by ignoring teachings about creation care. We can do this, first, because we believe that for every troubling issue we

2. Babylonian Talmud, tractate Shabbath 31a, The Soncino Edition, Brooklyn, NY, 1961. *https://ia700507.us.archive.org/12/items/TheBabylonianTalmudcompleteSoncinoEnglishTranslation/ The-Babylonian-Talmud-Complete-Soncino-English-Translation.pdf*

3. One could ask, do we need biblical cover for this element of coal mining? We would like to determine if our environmental practices harmonize with Scripture, and the chapter in Part I on "The Land" reveals that this practice does not.

confront, the Bible provides at least guidance, at best answers. In addition, we can do this because we are so numerous: 78.4 percent of American adults identify as Christians and 1.7 percent identify as Jews, according to the Pew Forum on Religion & Public Life. The adult population of the U.S. (age eighteen and over) exceeds 237 million, according to the Kids Count program of The Annie E. Casey Foundation. Even if only 10 percent of that number were to consider themselves people of faith, 19 million people constitute a powerful force for change.

If we seek biblical guidance about environmental problems, then we must return our attention to the opening books of the Bible. (Teachings about God's creation are found primarily in Genesis through Deuteronomy, for the writers of the Gospels and the Epistles sought to convey the life and teachings of Jesus and his disciples, not to rewrite the Law.) It is reasonable, therefore, for one primarily drawn to the Old Testament to offer a perspective, for both Christians and Jews, on the environmental-related teachings in the Law Jesus said he came to fulfill, to the books Jews call the Torah.

While epiphany may be too strong a description, my first jolt of awakening with the Bible came at age twelve. I encountered a verse in Leviticus 19 mandating that the land must be harvested in ways that leave food for the poor and the stranger. This was such an accessible instruction: It was easy to understand and made clear that following it would provide food for the needy and benefit the community as a whole. That verse about our use of the land created in me an indelible affinity for this text.

In that same year, and succeeding ones through age nineteen, I was drawn to many other passages that linked use of the land and care of the needy, that gave regulations about the treatment of animals, and that prohibited cutting down food-bearing trees even in time of war. Perhaps most striking was the requirement in the Ten Commandments to let our cattle also rest on the Sabbath.

The enduring connection signaled by my interest in environmental verses and a favorite pastime was not apparent at the time: I would often ride my bike to a hillside dense with trees that overlooked the Hudson River north of New York City and spend long stretches of time just sitting under a leafy canopy looking at the water. The trees afforded me privacy and protection, in contrast to the turbulence experienced elsewhere. Other times, I would bike for hours around the city, often taking long breaks by the river to feel transported by its movement and to look at the distant Palisades on the New Jersey side. This pattern of biblical inquiry and respite with the trees and river in my urban setting came to an abrupt end with the sudden death of my stepfather when I was nineteen. All my energy became focused on family needs and college courses.

By the mid-1980s, many years later, I was well into my professional career, having spent over a decade in aerospace engineering—working as what some now laughingly call a rocket scientist—and then made the transition to environmental work doing research on ways to minimize the heating, cooling, and lighting requirements of buildings. Except for a brief period of work exclusively in the computing industry, my professional career from the 1980s on involved energy and environmental issues, particularly how to reduce energy consumption in buildings and how improvements in building and appliance standards can reduce demands for electricity.

As well, by the mid-1980s, I returned to reviewing the large collection of verses about the land, animals, trees and, to my surprise, air, for pollution did exist in biblical times from tanneries and other sources. During this period, the national consciousness was gaining awareness of the gravity of environmental problems: The media had covered the Endangered Species Act, preserving biological diversity, recycling, the hole in the ozone layer, and CO_2 emissions that were leading to global warming, or what we now term climate change.

I began to think about whether this collection of biblical passages about the natural world related, in any explicit way, to current environmental problems. Not something tenuous, requiring a significant extrapolation from a verse, but explicitly. Where is something about recycling, air pollution, and endangered species? Concurrently, my analytical side was pushing me to gather together this collection of passages. That is, give a scientist a bunch of data, and one approach to understanding it is to see if the pieces fit together. Was there some core message, some overarching principle embodied in this collection of verses that spanned from Genesis to Deuteronomy?

Perhaps in a subconscious attempt to answer this question, I began offering talks in churches and synagogues about the Bible and the environment, some with friends who were ministers. When you teach, you learn.

Also at this time, I was a member of an organization whose mission was to urge members of churches and synagogues to align their personal and congregational activities in ways that harmonized with biblical teachings. In practice, our recommendations focused on building-energy audits, recycling, and organic gardening. We met with congregants and discussed the biblical connections to each of these. At several such meetings, when talking about care of the land, we heard the observation that from the perspective of Genesis 1:28, the earth is ours to use as we wish.

> God blessed them, and God said to them, "Be fruitful and multiply, and fill the earth and subdue it; and have dominion over the fish of the sea and over the birds of the air and over every living thing that moves upon the earth."

It is comforting to interpret Genesis 1:28 as calling for stewardship of the earth, someone would say, but that is not really what the verse says. The passage seems fairly clear with "subdue" and "have dominion over." When I'd point to a verse about a link between harvesting the land and care of the needy, or a requirement about the treatment of animals, the reply was generally, yes, we do need to take care of the hungry, or we should not be cruel to animals, but Genesis 1:28 gives us the natural world for our use.

This is a tremendously convenient perspective to have. We could engage in all kinds of activities with respect to our environment, and take biblical cover in "have dominion over."

The damaging consequences of this, and support for the perspective of these congregants, were eloquently spelled out in a 1966 talk and 1967 publication by the historian Lynn White Jr. titled "The Historical Roots of Our Ecologic Crisis."[4] White wrote that our failure to deal with the environmental crisis upon us has its roots in Genesis 1:28, from which he gathered the perspective that "no item in the physical creation had any purpose save to serve man's purposes." As a corollary, why would we have to change the way we exploit the natural world, despite the obvious damaging effects, if the Bible indicates it is ours to use as we wish?

I agreed that viewing the Genesis verse as a summary of the environmental teachings constituted a major obstacle to meaningful corrective actions. I did not agree, however, that Genesis 1:28 summed up the environmental mandate in the Torah. Rather, I saw it as simply the first of many passages about our interactions with the natural world. What guiding principle could we extract from a collective view?

It would be several years before I arrived at a reasonable formulation of that guiding principle, but not too long until one perspective on the collection of environmental teachings became clear. This view is given in detail in

---

4. From *Science*, Vol. 155, No. 3767, March 10, 1967, 1203–1207. Reprinted with permission from AAAS.

Part I, and builds on the idea that Genesis 1:28 is just the first of many environmental-related verses; some of the passages clarify earlier ones and others offer new instructions. When the teachings in Genesis–Deuteronomy are taken together, we have the material for a genuine biblical bottom line about our interaction with God's creation. That bottom line serves as an alternative to the Genesis 1:28 interpretation.

The review of the environmental passages in Genesis–Deuteronomy includes relating each to its contemporary form. For example, the teachings about air pollution connect now to CO_2 and climate change, with predictions that, in faith-based terminology, they will devastate God's creation and afflict first and hardest "the least of these."[5] I do not believe, therefore, that people can remain indifferent to the ravaging of creation and still call themselves persons of faith. We can't have it both ways.

People driven more by science than faith are already mobilizing to slow climate change, and are joined by many who see the spiritual imperative as well. If they were joined by large numbers of those driven more by faith than science, who would proclaim the spiritual case for ending reliance on fossil fuels for energy, we would strengthen the movement to slow climate change and preserve a hospitable planet. The expression "preserve a hospitable planet" is not used for dramatic purposes—the stakes are really that high.

Slowing climate change means transforming our society—indeed, the world—from one which relies on coal and oil for energy to one that uses the radiation from the sun, the power of the wind, and nuclear energy. Rightly so, this seems like an enormous undertaking, but it is underway in this country and many others. The problem lies with the pace of change—it is far too slow to avoid the devastation that higher temperatures, furious storms, droughts, and water shortages will bring to the planet. The slow pace results, primarily, from impediments put in place by major corporations and those they influence. This will connect, as we will find, to a crucial insight of the twentieth-century theologian Reinhold Niebuhr, a teaching that influenced the Rev. Martin Luther King, Jr.'s leadership of the civil rights movement, and that offers guidance about a successful environmental rights movement: "Individual men may be moral in the sense that they are able to consider interests other than their own in determining problems of conduct, and are capable, on occasion, of preferring the advantages of

---

5. Matthew 25:40.

others to their own. . . . But . . . these achievements are more difficult, if not impossible, for human societies and social groups."[6]

In order to extend and deepen the discussion of the biblical teachings covered in Part I, each chapter includes questions suitable for a teen or adult class.

Parts II and III of the book respond to the question of what, specifically, can individuals and non-governmental organizations do to accelerate the movement from fossil fuels to energy sources free of greenhouse gas emissions. We can do an enormous amount through both advocacy and personal actions. We can advocate for closing a coal-fired power plant; not cutting down a grove of trees; and choosing wind power to generate electricity, rather than installing another gas turbine plant.

In addition, the move to renewable energy, and to nuclear energy, can be accelerated by the personal actions we take. Part III offers a number of specific suggestions, such as reducing energy use in our homes and businesses by buying energy-efficient products and using them in a non-wasteful manner; by purchasing a hybrid car; and by installing photovoltaic solar panels to provide electricity.

People of faith, motivated by religious beliefs, can bring this country to the tipping point of full engagement with climate change. In 2015, we still have time, though with CO_2 levels continuing to climb, we can reach a point where a climate catastrophe becomes unavoidable. Imagine people paddling a canoe to avoid a waterfall toward which a strong current is carrying them. At some point, depending on the speed of the current and proximity to the falls, no matter how fast they paddle, they are going over. We do not want to reach that point. In Part II, we will review highly credible plans to slow climate change and to stabilize our climate.

But first we will uncover clear biblical teachings urging us to act. It is past time that we put our beliefs into action. That is why two sections of this book include "A Call to Action" in their titles. More pages are devoted to this than the biblical aspects, though at its heart the work aims to answer the *why* and *what* questions: Why should people of faith feel an obligation to take on climate change, and what specifically can we do? May this work promote both dialogue and action.

---

6. Reinhold Niebuhr, *Moral Man and Immoral Society* (New York: Charles Scribner's Sons, 1932), xi.

Part I

Environmental Teachings in the Bible
Jesus Knew

1

Invitation

The terms "ecological crisis" or "environmental problems" at heart refer to the troubled relationship between human beings and God's creation. At one end of that relationship are secular issues such as climate change, endangered species, and toxic wastes, and at the other end are biblical teachings about the interrelationships among God, people, and nature.

The biblical interrelationships involving God's creation are found primarily in the books Genesis through Deuteronomy, five books in the bibles of Christians and Jews. Some see the Bible as a text about God and a people, while it is rather a book about God, a people, and creation. The creation narrative occurs in Genesis, and the numerous aspects of the interrelationships between people and the created world are found in Genesis through Deuteronomy. If Christians and Jews seek biblical guidance about the environmental issues upon us, including climate change and its multiple ramifications, that guidance can be found most clearly in these five books.

Some, possibly surprising, examples include:

- Enabling cattle to rest on the Sabbath. In the Ten Commandments we find:

  > But the seventh day is a sabbath to the LORD your God; you shall not do any work—you, your son or your daughter, your male or female slave, your livestock, or the alien resident in your towns.
  >
  > Exod. 20:8–10;

- Not destroying food-bearing trees even in time of war:

  > If you besiege a town for a long time, making war against it in order to take it, you must not destroy its trees by wielding an axe against them. Although you may take food from them, you must not cut them down;
  >
  > Deut. 20:19

- Allowing an animal to eat when hungry:

  You shall not muzzle an ox while it is treading out the grain.

  Deut. 25:4;

- Connecting use of the land with obligations to the needy—it's not just take, take, take:

  > When you reap the harvest of your land, you shall not reap to the very edges of your field, or gather the gleanings of your harvest; you shall leave them for the poor and for the alien: I am the LORD your God.

  Lev. 23:22

We will examine these and other individual biblical commandments that relate to the environment. In addition, we will develop a *collective* view of those commandments in order to understand *our latitude with respect to the natural world*. That is, looking at all of these verses together, Part I offers a perspective on the biblically based freedom given to Christians and Jews to interact with the animals, birds, fish, trees, land, water, and air that comprise the world.

The Genesis 1:28 verse, "God blessed them, and God said to them, 'Be fruitful and multiply, and fill the earth and subdue it; and have dominion over the fish of the sea and over the birds of the air and over every living thing that moves upon the earth,'" has been interpreted as giving us great freedom with creation, as meaning we can do with the earth what we wish. But each time a verse such as one of the four above is encountered, it limits what we can do, and diminishes that freedom.

As we move from Genesis to Exodus to Leviticus to Numbers and finally to Deuteronomy and *develop a collective view* of the environmental teachings, that latitude steadily narrows. By the conclusion of Part I, we will discover how to formulate a biblically based synthesis corresponding to that resulting latitude.

That formulation, based on Genesis–Deuteronomy, would replace the one based on a single line in Genesis 1. Supplanting the idea that the earth and its resources are ours to use as we wish is vitally important. Some Christians and Jews look to the Bible as they form decisions about the appropriateness of human actions. A biblical teaching may not be the only criterion, but one of them. Yet, as long as we believe the Bible endorses a no-holds-barred attitude towards creation, we fail to bring an accurate biblical perspective to our decision-making process.

Some biblical commentators qualify their perspective by suggesting that Genesis 1:28 calls for stewardship of creation. While that appears reasonable, the interpretation must be inferred from the text, as it is not explicit in the verse. For people of faith who rely on explicit biblical teachings, the stewardship perspective may not carry persuasive force.

While this book is intended for Christians and Jews who hold the Bible sacred, the audience may be characterized in another way, given the recounting of God's words at the moment of revelation at Sinai:

> I am making this covenant, sworn by an oath, not only with you who stand here with us today before the LORD our God, but also with those who are not here with us today.
>
> Deut. 29:14–15

All of us were not standing physically at Sinai that day. It would appear, therefore, that God is continually offering this covenant to those not present at the historic Sinai. Each of us chooses to accept or decline this covenant. If we accept it, then we are part of the collective to whom the Bible speaks and the intended audience for this book.

Any reader questioning how a biblical inquiry can appeal to Christians and Jews equally, might be assuaged by the origin and meaning of the name "Israel": In the Jacob narrative in Genesis 32, Jacob prepares for a meeting with his estranged brother, Esau. Near nightfall, Jacob takes his wives, children, and possessions across the ford of the Jabbok River. The passage follows with: "Jacob was left alone; and a man wrestled with him until daybreak." These provocative verses conclude with the man saying:

> "What is your name?" And he said, "Jacob." Then the man said, "You shall no longer be called Jacob, but Israel, for you have striven with God and with humans, and have prevailed."
>
> Gen. 32:27–28

The name "Israel" denotes one who strives, wrestles with beings divine and human. Many Christians and Jews of faith see ourselves doing this, contending daily with earthly matters and concurrently striving to live in harmony with the divine, as best we can discern that.[1] Thus, the book's audience embraces equally all those who understand themselves as such wrestlers.

---

1. Rabbi Arthur Waskow indelibly characterized this striving in books titled *Godwrestling* and *Godwrestling Round 2*.

One of the issues with which we wrestle is climate change. The prevailing view asserts that climate change arises, at least in part, from emitting heat-trapping gases into the atmosphere through the burning of fossil fuels. Data recorded for more than fifty years reveal an undeniable buildup of carbon dioxide in the atmosphere. Carbon dioxide, methane, nitrous oxide, and other gases are heat-trapping, meaning that they reflect back to earth some of the heat that would normally vent into the atmosphere, just like the glass in a greenhouse reflects back into the building some of the heat that would otherwise escape into the air.

Evidence of this effect is both abundant and alarming:

- unprecedented melting of the polar ice caps, Greenland's ice sheet, and glaciers;
- increasing average temperature of the Earth over decades;
- changes in coral reefs and other marine life due to increasing water temperature;
- effects on migratory birds and marine life due to warmer air and water temperatures.

One additional predicted outcome is a rise in sea levels, which will adversely affect millions of people, animals, birds, and aquatic life that dwell in coastal regions, and entire island populations. Is there anything in the Bible that prescribes particular behavior regarding the release of gases and fumes that adversely affect others? Indeed, tanneries and other enterprises contributed to air pollution in ancient times, and we will see in later chapters the responses from religious authorities.

But when many Christians and Jews look to the Bible for instructions about our interactions with the natural world, we find it difficult to move past the Genesis 1:28 verse. That's our dominant view—that we rule God's creation and can do with it as we wish.

The historian Lynn White Jr., in a luminous 1966 address and 1967 publication titled *The Historical Roots of Our Ecologic Crisis*,[2] cited Genesis 1:28 as the root of our crisis. White wrote:

> . . . Christianity inherited from Judaism not only a concept of time as non-repetitive and linear but also a striking story of creation. By gradual stages a loving and all-powerful God had created light and darkness, the heavenly

---

2. *Science*, March 10, 1967, 1203–7.

bodies, the earth and all its plants, animals, birds, and fishes. Finally, God created Adam and, as an afterthought, Eve to keep man from being lonely. Man named all the animals, thus establishing his dominance over them. God planned all of this explicitly for man's benefit and rule: no item in the physical creation had any purpose save to serve man's purposes.

But Christianity inherited a Bible from Judaism, not just the opening chapters of Genesis. The "Law" for Jesus and for the writers of the Gospels was minimally Genesis–Deuteronomy, which contain a host of commandments regarding appropriate behavior with God's creation. The authors of the Gospels and the Epistles did not reformulate teachings in that area, but focused on the life and teachings of Jesus and his disciples.

With the focus in the Gospels on Jesus, and decisions by early church fathers that separated Christianity from Judaism (consider the names *Old* Testament and *New* Testament), the portions of the Bible that deal with our obligations to nature received less attention. The creation story itself remained compelling, and its concluding verse in Genesis 1:28 became the primary reference to the environment. In short, with this shift, Christianity lost touch with many teachings embraced by Jesus.[3] As we find in Matthew's recounting of the Sermon on the Mount:

> Do not think that I have come to abolish the law or the prophets; I have come not to abolish but to fulfil. For truly I tell you, until heaven and earth pass away, not one letter, not one stroke of a letter, will pass from the law until all is accomplished. Therefore, whoever breaks one of the least of these commandments, and teaches others to do the same, will be called least in the kingdom of heaven; but whoever does them and teaches them will be called great in the kingdom of heaven.
>
> Matt. 5:17–19a

This book takes the position that the laws of which Jesus spoke require renewed attention to guide the responses of Christians to the environmental crisis upon us. This does not mean that regardless of our present faith we begin following all these teachings, but that the clear understanding they express of the interdependence between humans and the natural world must shape our responses.

---

3. Lectionary readings do provide a continuing contact with "the Law," but do not generally stimulate study comparable to New Testament teachings.

While some American political leaders remain strongly influenced by the corporate energy sector, many citizens have been persuaded by the environmental damage that has occurred and predictions of what will occur from climate change. Perhaps people can be further motivated to engage this issue vigorously by becoming attentive to the laws Jesus sought to fulfill. By doing so, Christians and Jews find common cause and together advance creation care as part of their spiritual work in the world. A united effort by both faiths played a major role in establishing integration in America (after a slow start), and a joint effort could again have a transformative effect, this time upon the entire planet. Indeed, Part II does suggest another "rights" movement, an environmental rights movement, again led by clergy and driven by people of faith to save our world from the most destructive consequences of climate change.

DISCUSSION QUESTIONS

1. Discuss how the author broadens the audience for the book. Would you find yourself comfortable in this conversation regardless of your religious affiliation?
2. How does the expression "God wrestlers" affect your understanding of the name "Israel"?
3. Discuss your interpretation of Genesis 1:28.
4. Discuss the quotes from Lynn White Jr.'s essay and the author's comments.

2

Interpretation and Translation

The English verbs translated from the Hebrew in Genesis 1:28 as "subdue" and "have dominion over" understandably suggest free rein, as giving humankind much autonomy with respect to the environment. We can do with the earth what we wish. The intent of the original Hebrew, however, is less clear.

The Hebrew word translated as "subdue" is *ke'vosh*, which can indeed mean to subdue, or bring into bondage, to press, or to squeeze. The word *ke'vosh* is used today to express, for example, how a metal smith hammers copper into shape, or how a steamroller presses tar into a roadbed. This usage suggests that "to press," "to shape," or "to form" more clearly reveal what is meant than "subdue." These verbs appear more in harmony with the instructions about the Garden given in Genesis 2, "to till it and to tend it," than "subdue" or "master."

This first instance of a cautious approach to an English translation of a Hebrew word serves as a reminder of the uncertainty inherent in any version of the Bible. Figures 1A and 1B depict the opening passages of Leviticus 19, part of the Holiness Code.[1] Figure 1A shows the text as it appears in the Torah, the foundational text for Jewish and Christian scripture. This root version contains no vowels and no punctuation. Readers of this scroll need to discern where one word ends and the next begins and, to use English for illustration, whether the letters *mstr* mean master, mister, or muster. Figure 1B shows the same section as it appears in printed texts, with vowels and punctuation.

---

1. Verse 19:2 includes, "You shall be holy, for I the LORD your God am holy." This chapter of Leviticus then provides numerous instructions for behaviors required for holiness.

The evolution of the first five books into the forms now familiar to Christians and Jews included three major steps. The first step resulted in the Septuagint, a translation of the Hebrew Bible (as seen in Figure 1A) into Greek that was completed by Jewish scholars around 200 BCE, primarily to accommodate the Jews who no longer spoke Hebrew. The Septuagint represents an *interpretation* of the core Hebrew Bible, for vowel decisions have been made and words separated. That does not mean that those choices were the only ones possible, or that other punctuation choices could not alter the meaning.

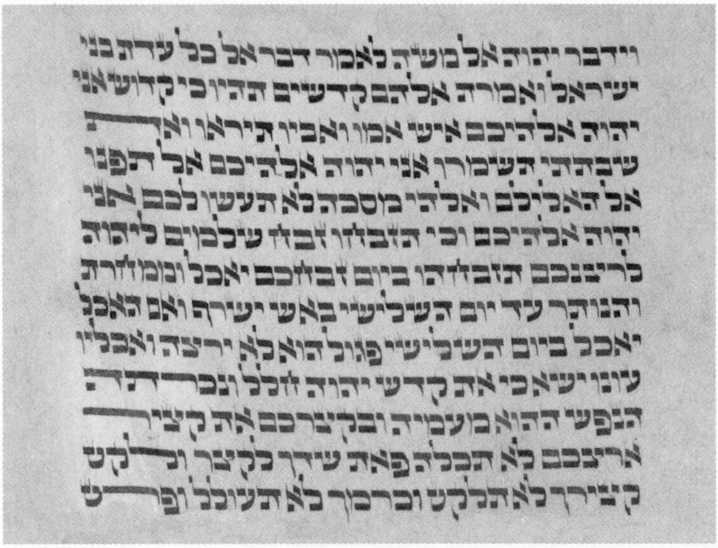
וידבר יהוה אל משה לאמר דבר אל כל עדת בני
ישראל ואמרת אלהם קדשים תהיו כי קדוש אני
יהוה אלהיכם איש אמו ואביו תיראו ואת
שבתתי תשמרו אני יהוה אלהיכם אל תפנו
אל האלילם ואלהי מסכה לא תעשו לכם אני
יהוה אלהיכם וכי תזבחו זבח שלמים ליהוה
לרצנכם תזבחהו ביום זבחכם יאכל וממחרת
והנותר עד יום השלישי באש ישרף ואם האכל
יאכל ביום השלישי פגול הוא לא ירצה ואכליו
עונו ישא כי את קדש יהוה חלל ונכרתה ה
הנפש ההוא מעמיה ובקצרכם את קציר
ארצכם לא תכלה פאת שדך לקצר ולקט
קצירך לא תלקט וכרמך לא תעולל ופרט

Figure 1A

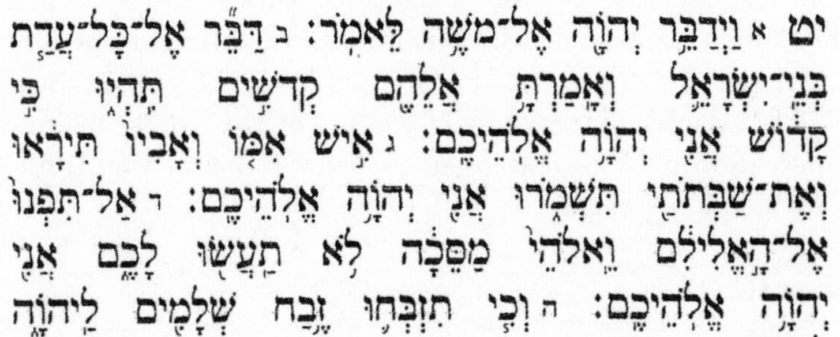
יט א וַיְדַבֵּר יְהוָה אֶל־מֹשֶׁה לֵּאמֹר׃ ב דַּבֵּר אֶל־כָּל־עֲדַת
בְּנֵי־יִשְׂרָאֵל וְאָמַרְתָּ אֲלֵהֶם קְדֹשִׁים תִּהְיוּ כִּי
קָדוֹשׁ אֲנִי יְהוָה אֱלֹהֵיכֶם׃ ג אִישׁ אִמּוֹ וְאָבִיו תִּירָאוּ
וְאֶת־שַׁבְּתֹתַי תִּשְׁמֹרוּ אֲנִי יְהוָה אֱלֹהֵיכֶם׃ ד אַל־תִּפְנוּ
אֶל־הָאֱלִילִם וֵאלֹהֵי מַסֵּכָה לֹא תַעֲשׂוּ לָכֶם אֲנִי
יְהוָה אֱלֹהֵיכֶם׃ ה וְכִי תִזְבְּחוּ זֶבַח שְׁלָמִים לַיהוָה
לִרְצֹנְכֶם תִּזְבָּחֻהוּ׃ ו בְּיוֹם זִבְחֲכֶם יֵאָכֵל וּמִמָּחֳרָת

Figure 1B

The Vulgate is a translation from the Hebrew into Latin that was completed in the fourth century CE by St. Jerome. In a similar fashion, vowel and meaning choices have been made with the Vulgate.

Lastly, the Masoretic text is a scholarly standardization of the original unvocalized (that is, vowel-less) Hebrew into Hebrew with vowels and punctuation, and was compiled in the seventh to tenth centuries. These three comprise the core interpretative works from which subsequent translations derived.

The ambiguity inherent in the original Hebrew (Fig. 1A) remains. Readers would benefit, therefore, by remaining mindful that contemporary printed Scripture contains a degree of uncertainty over and above any that results from biblical exegesis, that is, spiritual interpretation.

That uncertainty manifests with the opening verse of Genesis 1. The first word Jews read as *B'reishit* is grammatically puzzling; it's unclear how to translate it. The commentary on this verse in *The Torah: A Modern Commentary* states that "Our translation [When God was about to create] follows Rashi,[2] who said that the first word would have been written *ba-rishona* [rather than *B'reishit*, at first], if its primary purpose had been to teach the order in which creation took place."[3] Thus, some versions of Genesis open with "When God began to create . . ." and others use "In the beginning . . ." We cannot faithfully or conclusively render into English what the author of Genesis meant to express with even the first word.

Puzzles continue with the second and third words, a verb in singular form and its subject, a noun in plural form. That is, the word translated as "God" is *Elohim*, which is in the plural. Scholars believe that by the time this was written down, the people saw God as One, but the grammatical inconsistency in the original Hebrew remains.

Historical records indicate that for centuries people assembled to hear the Torah read out loud. Over the years, different speakers likely made different choices about the pronunciation of various words. The Masorites produced a standardized version of the Torah, making vowel and punctuation choices that retained every letter of the Torah in the order in which it appeared.

---

2. Rabbi Shlomo Yitzchaki (known by the acronym Rashi) was the preeminent commentator on the Bible and the Talmud during the Middle Ages. He was born in Troyes, France, in 1040 and died in 1105.

3. W. Gunther Plaut, ed., David E. S. Stein, ed. revised edition, *The Torah: A Modern Commentary* (New York: URJ Press, 2005), 19.

As biblical verses are cited and interpretations offered, I acknowledge knowing that other readers can extract subtle to significant differences in meaning. Most of the interpretations given in this book benefit from being derivative of what others have offered over centuries of study and therefore suggest a mainstream viewpoint.

The novelty of the approach taken here derives from the synthesis that will develop by viewing *collectively* the biblical teachings regarding actions with respect to creation. The successive commandments encountered as one moves from Genesis to Deuteronomy become a series of constraints that narrow our latitude with respect to the natural world. Genesis 1:28 serves as a starting point and indeed gives wide latitude with respect to the environment, but that scope diminishes markedly by the conclusion of Deuteronomy.

The expansive interpretation of Genesis 1:28 becomes doubtful as soon as we encounter the Noah story in Genesis 7. We turn to that next.

DISCUSSION QUESTIONS

1. What does it suggest to you that the Torah contains no vowels and no punctuation? Discuss the uncertainty the author illustrates with the first three words of the Torah.

2. How might your understanding of the opening creation story of Genesis change if you read the first words as "In the beginning . . ." or "When God began to create . . ."?

3

Noah and Biodiversity

The narrative about Noah and the flood spans chapters 7–9 of Genesis and offers teachings applicable to a contemporary environmental issue. In Genesis 7, God tells Noah that He will bring a flood to destroy all life on earth, and that Noah should build an ark to accommodate Noah's family and pairs of all animals and birds. The section reads:

> Then the LORD said to Noah, "Go into the ark, you and all your household, for I have seen that you alone are righteous before me in this generation. Take with you seven pairs of all clean animals, the male and its mate; and a pair of the animals that are not clean, the male and its mate; and seven pairs of the birds of the air also, male and female, to keep their kind alive on the face of all the earth. For in seven days I will send rain on the earth for forty days and forty nights; and every living thing that I have made I will blot out from the face of the ground." And Noah did all that the LORD had commanded him.
>
> Gen. 7:1–5

Note the closing verse. Noah had no discretion about what to place in the ark. If Noah was to "fill the earth and subdue it; and have dominion over the fish of the sea and over the birds of the air and over every living thing that moves upon the earth" as "have dominion over" has been interpreted, God could have told Noah to select land animals and birds to place in the ark. The flood episode could have been written that way, and we would understand that the species that survived the flood did so because of Noah's decisions. But that is not the narrative: "And Noah did all that the Lord had commanded him."

I suggest that Genesis 7 fundamentally undermines the prevailing, expansive interpretation of Genesis 1:28. In this instance and elsewhere that we shall encounter, God reveals the limits of our latitude, our mastery.

The Noah story in Genesis 7–9 gives Christians and Jews additional powerful insights into appropriate behavior with respect to animals, fish, and birds. The opening verses of Genesis 7 make clear that all animals and birds were to board the ark with Noah and his family. In one of the rare (and therefore important) instances of repetition in Torah, we find such directions given also in Genesis 6:19–20, and Genesis 7:8–9.

> And of every living thing, of all flesh, you shall bring two of every kind into the ark, to keep them alive with you; they shall be male and female. Of the birds according to their kinds, and of the animals according to their kinds, of every creeping thing of the ground according to its kind, two of every kind shall come in to you, to keep them alive.
>
> Gen. 6:19–20

Genesis 7:8, 9 indicates the fulfillment of that precise command:

> Of clean animals, and of animals that are not clean, and of birds, and of everything that creeps on the ground, two and two, male and female, went into the ark with Noah, as God had commanded Noah.
>
> Gen. 7:8, 9

The repetitions make clear that God intended to preserve all species. Accordingly, this section has been cited by scholars as a proof text for preserving biological diversity.[1] If God required all species to survive, then humans have no license to willfully contribute to the demise of a species. We know, however, that for a variety of reasons, many species have been lost over the years.[2]

In the early 1970s, leaders at the federal level began to understand the cascading effects of species loss, and with the realization that the population of the bald eagle, our national symbol, had dwindled to a dangerous level, Congress took action. In 1973, Congress passed the Endangered Species Act (ESA), and in that same year the law underwent a crucial test in the case of the snail darter.

---

1. See, for example, Jeremy Benstein, *The Way Into Judaism and the Environment* (Woodstock, VT: Jewish Lights Publishing, 2006).

2. Species that humans have hunted to extinction include: dodo bird; passenger pigeon; Carolina parakeet; and the Tasmanian tiger. Among the currently endangered species due to climate change are: polar bear; grizzly bear; Kauai creeper bird (a type of honeycreeper); elkhorn coral; bull trout; and Pacific salmon. Information about endangered species was obtained from the Environmental News Service: *www.ens-newswire.com/ens/dec2009/2009-12-01-091.asp*. Particularly disturbing is the finding published in *Audubon*, March–April 2014, that 314 species of North American birds are at risk of extinction from climate change.

Construction of the Tellico Dam on the Little Tennessee River began in 1967, and by 1973 was about 90 percent complete. In August of 1973, Professor David Etneir of the University of Tennessee discovered the snail darter[3] in the Little Tennessee River while doing research related to a lawsuit involving the National Environmental Policy Act (NEPA). The lawsuit claimed that the Tellico Reservoir, which would result from the dam, would render the snail darter extinct. Up to this point, the NEPA lawsuit had slowed construction of the dam, but not halted it.

The case eventually reached the Supreme Court, and in 1978 the Court ruled that the ESA prohibited the completion of the Tellico Dam if it would likely result in the loss of a species.

The ruling created quite a controversy in Congress, and led to the passage of an amendment that called for the creation of a committee, sometimes called the God Committee, with the power to exempt a project from the ESA. Congress believed this would resolve the Tellico controversy.

The committee took up the Tellico project and eventually voted unanimously in favor of the snail darter. They did so, however, on economic grounds, not ecological ones. That still did not conclude the issue.

Senator Howard Baker of Tennessee, after an earlier unsuccessful effort, eventually secured the passage in 1979 of an amendment to the ESA that exempted Tellico from the law.

Prior to the closing of the gates on the Tellico Dam, numerous snail darters were moved into the Hiwassee River, where they flourished. In November 1979, the Tennessee Valley Authority closed the gates on the Tellico Dam, and in the 1980s the snail darter was removed from the ESA.[4]

The snail darter saga illustrates that in a conflict between an endangered species and development, we can, in some cases, find a way to satisfy both objectives. In the snail darter case, adherence to the law and imaginative thinking resolved the conflict. We need such patience and justice to routinely characterize our actions.

The flood episode represents a new beginning for the earth, one that will be launched by those on board the ark. If we contrast the blessing God gave to Noah and his sons with the blessing in Genesis 1 given to the first humans, we find a striking difference. Genesis 9 opens with:

---

3. The snail darter is a two- to three-inch speckled brown fish with a blunt snout, eyes placed toward the top of its head, and four dorsal saddles, or bands, across the back. Its diet consists mainly of aquatic snails and insects.

4. Information on the Tellico Dam history was obtained from "The Snail Darter versus Tellico Dam." *http://www.mhhe.com/Enviro-Sci/CaseStudyLibrary/Topic-Based/CaseStudy_TheSnailDarterVersus.pdf*

God blessed Noah and his sons, and said to them, "Be fruitful and multi-ply, and fill the earth. The fear and dread of you shall rest on every animal of the earth, and on every bird of the air, on everything that creeps on the ground, and on all the fish of the sea; into your hand they are delivered. Every moving thing that lives shall be food for you; and just as I gave you the green plants, I give you everything."

Gen. 9:1–3

Thus, the Genesis 1:28 instruction to "Be fruitful and multiply, and fill the earth and subdue it; and have dominion over the fish of the sea . . ." has changed to "Be fruitful and multiply, and fill the earth. The fear and dread of you shall rest on every animal of the earth. . . into your hand they are delivered." Humans now induce fear and dread in everything with which the earth is astir. Our relationship has been dramatically re-characterized, with the Genesis 1:28 instruction left behind. This finding at the end of the Noah story joins with our observation at the beginning of the flood episode that Noah's ability to "*have dominion over*" did not even extend to selecting the types or numbers of creatures of the air and land that were to board the ark: "And Noah did all that the LORD had commanded him."

Thus, these bookends to the flood narrative seem to limit the prevail-ing interpretation of Genesis 1:28 to the Garden of Eden. This conclusion gains validity as we encounter verse after verse in Genesis–Deuteronomy that provide instructions for our interactions with the natural world, and in no instance suggest that we can simply do as we wish—no holds barred.

The opening of Genesis 9 changes our relationship with other crea-tures, first, it appears, by stating that "Every moving thing that lives shall be food for you" (which differs from Genesis 1:29) and, implicitly, because our actions will determine their existence and impinge on their sense of safety and wellbeing. Deuteronomy, in addition, contains several verses that con-strain our actions towards other forms of life.

Genesis 9 continues with God establishing a covenant with all life on earth, with a rainbow serving as a sign of the covenant "that never again shall all flesh be cut off by the waters of a flood, and never again shall there be a flood to destroy the earth" (Gen. 9:11).

The Noah section opened with repeated phrases revealing the divine intent to preserve all life forms on earth, and closes with repeated phrases revealing that the covenant is established with *all* life on earth, not just with humans. Consider:

God said, "This is the sign of the covenant that I make between me and you and every living creature that is with you, for all future generations: I have set my bow in the clouds, and it shall be a sign of the covenant between me and the earth."

Gen. 9:12–13

"I will remember my covenant that is between me and you and every living creature of all flesh; and the waters shall never again become a flood to destroy all flesh. When the bow is in the clouds, I will see it and remember the everlasting covenant between God and every living creature of all flesh that is on the earth." God said to Noah, "This is the sign of the covenant that I have established between me and all flesh that is on the earth."

Gen. 9:15–17

These verses reveal:

- That God makes the first covenant with all life-forms equally, not just with humans;
- That presumably the ant, the camel, and the robin are as aware of this covenant as we are—perhaps by seeing the bow in the clouds, perhaps by other means. A covenant requires an awareness by both parties of the terms of the agreement, thus asking us to consider what it means that our dog or cat holds this awareness.

If such an awareness seems far-fetched, consider one of the biblical stories rich with interpretative possibilities, the tale of Balak and Balaam found in Numbers 22. The king of Moab, Balak, has persuaded Balaam, who we are told communicates with God, to come and curse the Israelites camped adjacent to his land. Balak views them as a threat and believes he will be able to defeat them if they are weakened by Balaam's curse.

En route to Balak, Balaam's donkey sees an angel of God standing on the road with sword drawn. The donkey changes course to avoid the angel and is struck by Balaam. This happens a second time. On the third encounter, the angel maneuvers the donkey into a narrow path from which she cannot proceed, and the donkey sits down. This prompts several angry blows from Balaam. Then God gives the donkey the ability to speak and she says, in I imagine a snarky tone, "Am I not your donkey, which you have ridden all your life to this day? Have I been in the habit of treating you this way?" Balaam replies "No." Then God enables Balaam to see the angel and the reason for the donkey's behavior becomes clear.

The text says "The donkey saw the angel of the LORD standing in the road, with a drawn sword in his hand." Thus, we are told that the donkey was able to see the angel without divine intervention. In contrast, the text says "Then the LORD opened the eyes of Balaam, and he saw the angel of the LORD standing in the road, with his drawn sword in his hand." Balaam, who communicates with God, could only see the angel when God enabled him to (Num. 22:31).

The text invites us to speculate then, that some animals (who can perceive smells and sights humans cannot) have abilities that extend to observing divine messengers and, perhaps, knowing the terms of the covenant after the flood; in Hebrew, the word for messenger is the same as the word for angel (*malach*).

The story continues with the angel allowing Balaam to proceed, but cautions him, as God did before he left, only to direct words to the encamped Israelites that he will convey to him. The words Balaam eventually speaks, to the dismay of King Balak, are found in Numbers 24:5 and in Jewish liturgy: "how fair are your tents, O Jacob, your encampments, O Israel!"

Toward the end of the Lynn White essay quoted in chapter 1, he writes, "Hence we shall continue to have a worsening ecologic crisis until we reject the Christian axiom that nature has no reason for existence save to serve man."[5]

White's prediction partly motivates this book. While I do not agree with White's assertion about a Christian axiom, I do believe it is a premise of Western civilization of which Christianity is the dominant religion. That axiom, White says, derives from Genesis 1:28. This chapter is revealing that the collection of verses in Genesis–Deuteronomy that limit our interactions with nature demonstrate how that premise of Western civilization can impede action on climate change. If "nature has no reason for existence save to serve" us, why was the first covenant made with all life on earth, why did God require saving all species during the flood, and why did God give the Sabbath to our cattle? I believe we can reject the premise that has for so long characterized Western thinking about the natural world.

As long as our reactions to climate change are dominated by short-term concerns, particularly financial, we bequeath to our children and grandchildren an increasingly hostile world and an increasing financial burden to deal with the effects of climate change. If Christians and Jews cannot be motivated by love for our descendants, perhaps we can be motivated by contemplating that our inattention to creation-related teachings may distance us from the divine.

---

5. *Science*, March 10, 1967, 1203–7.

DISCUSSION QUESTIONS

1. How do you view the applicability of Genesis 7 to the goal of preserving biological diversity?
2. What is your view of the history of Tellico Dam and the snail darter?
3. Discuss the effects of a loss of a species. Do we need to try to save all species?
4. Describe the covenant God makes with Noah and all life on earth and your thoughts about the inclusiveness of that covenant.
5. To what degree do you see climate change as damaging God's creation?
6. Discuss whether you see climate change as a religious/spiritual issue.

4

Paying Attention

Simply manifesting an awareness of climate change may be seen as a holy act, for it connects us to one of the key phrases in our shared biblical heritage, Deuteronomy 6:4: "Hear, O Israel: The LORD is our God, the LORD alone." The phrase "Hear, O Israel" comes from the Hebrew *Shema Yisrael*, and may be translated as "Hear, O Israel," "Listen, O Israel," or colloquially, "Pay attention, God-wrestlers!" Scripture commands us to pay attention. Indeed, Jesus cites the first two lines of the *Shema* as the most important commandment:

> One of the scribes came near and . . . he asked him, "Which commandment is the first of all?" Jesus answered, "The first is, 'Hear, O Israel: the Lord our God, the Lord is one; you shall love the Lord your God with all your heart, and with all your soul, and with all your mind, and with all your strength.'"
>
> Mark 12:28–30 (See also Matt. 22:37; Luke 10:25–28)

The last letter in the word *shema* in this verse, the Hebrew letter *ayin*, is written larger than other letters in both the Torah and most prayer books. Similarly, the last letter (*dalet*) in the final word, one (*echad*), is usually written larger in the Torah and most prayer books.

These two letters command a reader's attention and, taken together, form the Hebrew word for "witness." Even by means of calligraphy, Christians and Jews are commanded to witness this phrase, to witness what is in the Bible, to observe and pay attention to what we see, hear, and experience.

The prophet Isaiah offers a compelling corollary from the word "witness:" "You are my witnesses, says the LORD, and my servant whom I have chosen" (Isa. 43:10). The power of this becomes clear if we consider the opposite of this teaching: "If you are my witnesses, I am the Lord, and if

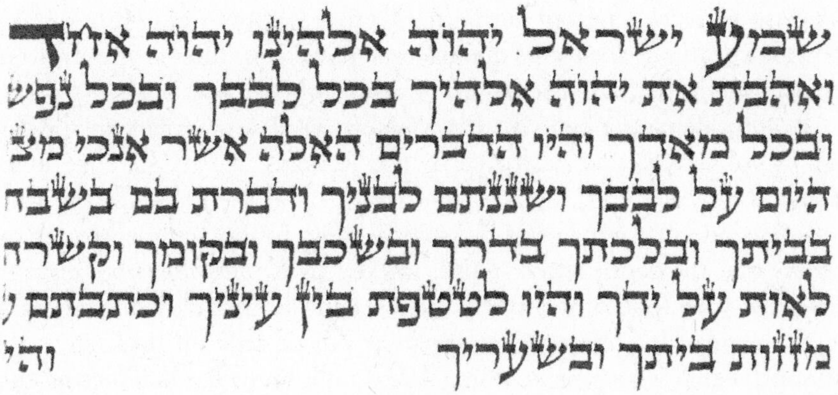

שְׁמַע יִשְׂרָאֵל יְהוָה אֱלֹהֵינוּ יְהוָה אֶחָד
וְאָהַבְתָּ אֵת יְהוָה אֱלֹהֶיךָ בְּכָל לְבָבְךָ וּבְכָל נַפְשְׁךָ
וּבְכָל מְאֹדֶךָ וְהָיוּ הַדְּבָרִים הָאֵלֶּה אֲשֶׁר אָנֹכִי מְצַ
הַיּוֹם עַל לְבָבֶךָ וְשִׁנַּנְתָּם לְבָנֶיךָ וְדִבַּרְתָּ בָּם בְּשִׁבְתְּ
בְּבֵיתֶךָ וּבְלֶכְתְּךָ בַּדֶּרֶךְ וּבְשָׁכְבְּךָ וּבְקוּמֶךָ וּקְשַׁרְתָּ
לְאוֹת עַל יָדֶךָ וְהָיוּ לְטֹטָפֹת בֵּין עֵינֶיךָ וּכְתַבְתָּם ּ
מְזֻזוֹת בֵּיתֶךָ וּבִשְׁעָרֶיךָ וְהָיּ

Figure 2

you are not my witnesses, I am not, as it were, the Lord."[1] That is, we participate in a reciprocal relationship, with our not witnessing God effectively removing God from our lives.

Scripture invites us into a relationship with the Creator; the Creator directs us to care for creation. Climate change is presenting us with irrefutable evidence of damage to God's creation. Do we choose to pay attention to what we observe in the natural world largely as a result of our actions and respond, or do we choose not to witness it and accordingly take no action?

We are God's witnesses, and we are called to action. The second section of this book covers one actionable blueprint for stabilizing earth's climate. It will take faith and determination to implement it. Let us, at least, manifest such faith.

People of faith can wield enormous influence, for about 190 million American adults identify as Christians or Jews. Surely the combination of the physical evidence we observe, the consensus of the scientific community, and the biblical teachings we look to can move us to action.

The actions will result in change, moving from fossil fuels for energy to renewables and nuclear energy. Those with a strong interest in the status quo are resisting that change, even though their resistance means harming the global community of which we are a part and eroding the habitability of the planet. Those consequences challenge our instinct for self-preservation

---

1. William G. Braude, ed., Pesikta Derab Kahana (Philadelphia: Jewish Publication Society, 2002), 414. [The teaching was likely written somewhere between the seventh and tenth centuries.]

and clash with the tenets of our faith. It is that support—our faith—against which advocates of the status quo become powerless. That is why, from my perspective, the active participation of people of faith is crucial.

In Jerusalem, one can visit the Western Wall, a boundary of the Second Temple compound destroyed by the Romans in 70 CE. The Temple Mount is now home to the Al-Aqsa Mosque and the Dome of the Rock. If you ascend what remains of the steps leading to the Temple Mount, you observe that the depth of the steps is uneven. Some provide about eighteen inches for your foot, others thirty inches, and the variations in step depth are not regular. It's immediately apparent as you walk up these steps that you must watch what you are doing. We do not know the builder's motivation for that design, but it remains as evidence that it ensured the *attention*

Figure 3. Steps to the Temple Mount (Photo taken by author)

of those ascending to the Temple Mount, and it reminds us today of that core teaching.

While the desire to focus our attention when ascending the steps to the Temple seems obvious, I suggest that the phrase in Deuteronomy (*Shema, Israel*: "Listen, Israel") stands both alone as a command and as a prelude to the teaching that God is one. As Christians and Jews pay attention or manifest awareness of the changes on our planet, we connect with that imperative in Deuteronomy.

This brief review of environmental teachings in Genesis has revealed:

- That applying the broad interpretation of Genesis 1:28 to the rest of the Pentateuch appears inaccurate in light of both Noah's role in selecting animals for the ark *as God commanded him* and by the opening verses of Genesis 9 which gives a new characterization of the human-animal relationship with "the fear and the dread of you";
- That God makes the first covenant in the Bible with all living things equally, not just with humans;
- That we find both a biblical and historical requirement to witness, to pay attention, to be mindful when seeking a connection to God.

Our behavior with respect to the natural world as an integral part of our connection to, or disconnect from, God is reinforced when we review verses dealing with the treatment of animals.

DISCUSSION QUESTIONS

1. Discuss the importance of the *shema* to both Jews and Christians.
2. What do you think about the importance of paying attention? How does that manifest itself in practice?

5

Treatment of Animals

The books of Exodus, Leviticus, Numbers, and Deuteronomy contain numerous commandments concerning the treatment of animals. The frequency of these instructions is not surprising, given that the ancient Israelites were predominantly an agricultural people. Many were shepherds who understood the reciprocal relationship between their wellbeing and that of their flocks. They also saw that animals feel and express pain and that a strong bond exists between a mother animal and her offspring.

They also recognized that when an animal is offered to God it must be done with the right intentionality, and therefore requires an animal free of blemishes or mutilations.

The fourth commandment in the Decalogue in Exodus bears repeating in this context.

> Remember the sabbath day, and keep it holy. Six days you shall labor and do all your work. But the seventh day is a sabbath to the LORD your God; you shall not do any work—you, your son or your daughter, your male or female slave, your livestock, or the alien resident in your towns.
>
> Exod. 20:8–10

This verse in Exodus instructs the people to refrain from working their livestock on the Sabbath, just as they must refrain from work. We need to consider what it means to us, urbanites and farmers included, in the twenty-first century that the Bible restricts the use of cattle on the Sabbath. The commentary on Exodus 20:10 in *The Torah: A Modern Commentary* states that "Animals here receive the benefit of a legal enactment." This comment is a reminder of the covenantal relationship that animals have with God, as expressed in Genesis 9 in the covenant God made with all life on earth after the flood.

It is also profoundly important to recall the instruction to do no work on the Sabbath, for such observance can motivate us to care for creation. Recall an opening verse of Genesis 2, part of the creation narrative:

> So God blessed the seventh day and hallowed it, because on it God rested from all the work that he had done in creation.

Gen. 2:3

In remembrance of God resting after the work of creation, we are instructed to do no work on the seventh day. That remembrance can take many forms, including:

- Pausing to enjoy the natural beauty and diversity of the world we inherited. In distant times, the pause reminded our ancestors of the links between God, the natural world, and our permitted use of that world. In our time, the pause can do the same while making us less willing to be complicit in its devastation—ideally, to use our intelligence and strength to oppose the forces bringing irreparable damage to our livable world;
- Engaging in religious services that connect us with texts providing instructions about living in relation with God, each other, and the natural world.

More than ever, because the stakes are higher, we need to move from a 24/7 world to a 24/6 one, as Matthew Sleeth phrased it.[1] It is easy to remain digitally connected to our work, but such connection does not necessarily bring fulfillment or happiness. Rather, in part, it brings an inflated sense of self-importance and with it perhaps the delusion of immortality—we must be too important to leave this world. While such constant connection is appealing, with it we lose sight of what is truly vital. A conscious observance of the Sabbath is a necessary, though not sufficient, element of creation care, for the Sabbath and creation are inextricably linked. For that reason, let me touch on a personal perspective on the Sabbath.

While Jewish tradition proposes a set of do's and do not's for that day, extrapolated from activities required to construct the Tabernacle, my personal practice links back to the verse, "you shall do no work." I know what is work for me and what is pleasure, and on the Sabbath I avoid the former.

---

1. Matthew Sleeth, *24/6* (Carol Stream, IL: Tyndale House, 2012).

In the laws of *kashrut*,[2] food is classified as meat, dairy, or pareve—neither meat nor dairy, for example, vegetables. I imagine analogous categories with respect to activities: work, pleasure, or neutral.

For me, neutral includes flipping a light switch or heating some soup. Work includes engaging in an activity that is part of my employment, a task for which I receive compensation, or one that may be necessary but tedious, such as doing the laundry or shopping for groceries. Pleasure, for me, includes socializing with friends, listening to music, reading, and resting.

I view each such list as unique to the individual. For a person who enjoys woodworking, that might be a pleasurable Sabbath activity, whereas someone who views that as laborious would avoid it on the Sabbath.

To start the weekend looking forward to one day on which I will not do what I understand as work is tremendously liberating and restorative. Through observance, one can join that continuum of over twenty centuries of people who have followed the teachings of that verse, pausing to reflect on creation and to express gratitude, and perhaps stepping outside to enjoy it.

The books of Leviticus and Deuteronomy impose additional limits upon actions with respect to animals. For example, Leviticus 22:26–28 states:

> The LORD spoke to Moses, saying: When an ox or a sheep or a goat is born, it shall remain for seven days with its mother, and from the eighth day onwards it shall be acceptable as the LORD's offering by fire. But you shall not slaughter, from the herd or the flock, an animal with its young on the same day.
>
> Lev. 22:26–28

This resonates with our understanding of animals as sentient beings, not the commodities of factory farming, and exhibits a concern for the bond between a mother and her offspring. A commentary on Leviticus 22:26–28 states that "Humane feelings forbid unnecessary cruelty to animals."[3]

This passage and another we will encounter in Deuteronomy invite us to consider the relevance of a biblical point of view on:

---

2. These laws cover what animals, birds, and fish may be a source of food, and what may not; the regulations are discussed at some length in a later chapter.

3. *The Torah: A Modern Commentary*, 823.

- The methods for slaughtering animals for human consumption;
- The practice of using animals for product safety testing (now much reduced);
- Medical experimentation on animals;
- The practices of factory farming; and,
- The treatment of marine life, from high-amplitude sonar signals that injure and sometimes kill whales and dolphins, to the despicable practice of stripping the fins off sharks and tossing them, live but maimed, back into the water.

Deuteronomy 22 and 25 offer four additional teachings from which one could likely assemble book-length texts of the commentaries made upon them over the centuries. The objective here is only to highlight one aspect that comes through each instruction.

> You shall not see your neighbor's donkey or ox fallen on the road and ignore it; you shall help to lift it up.
>
> Deut. 22:4

One helps because both the neighbor and the animal need assistance, not solely for the sake of the neighbor.

> If you come on a bird's nest, in any tree or on the ground, with fledglings or eggs, with the mother sitting on the fledglings or on the eggs, you shall not take the mother with the young. Let the mother go, taking only the young for yourself, in order that it may go well with you and you may live long.
>
> Deut. 22:6–7

Not taking both the mother and the young enables the generations to continue. This instruction reverberates with the values of not contributing to the extinction of a species and preserving biological diversity, contemporary environmental issues rooted in Genesis 6 and 7 in the Noah section. The phrase "in order that it may go well with you and you may live long" signals both the forceful intent of this instruction and our interconnectedness with the wellbeing of other life forms and our responsibility to them.

> You shall not plough with an ox and a donkey yoked together.
>
> Deut. 22:10

This teaching prohibits harnessing together animals of vastly different strengths.

> You shall not muzzle an ox while it is treading out the grain.
>
> Deut. 25:4

The instruction in this verse enables the ox to eat when on the threshing floor, with grain all around. This avoids causing distress to the animal and exhibits respect for its basic needs.

Collectively, these teachings further narrow any broad view we held of the words "have dominion over" in Genesis 1:28. The next chapter considers contemporary practices that violate this tradition, those of factory farming and its parallels in the fishing industry, and the high penalty we might be paying for such practices.

DISCUSSION QUESTIONS

1. Have you thought about how the way animals are raised and slaughtered affects you as a consumer?

2. Have you found any Old or New Testament teachings relating to the quality of life and manner of death of animals?

3. What are some of the reasons people are vegetarians?

6

We Feel Their Pain

The passages in chapter 5 concerning compassionate behavior toward animals gave rise to a Jewish tradition called "concern for the distress of living creatures." That is, when scholars looked collectively at the commandments concerning animals, they concluded that the first five books of the Bible require that we not cause distress to living creatures and relieve their pain whenever it is observed. It has been argued that the intent of the laws of *kashrut* suffer in practice by focusing on the draining of blood after slaughter, while remaining inattentive to the physical and psychological pain animals endure during their lifetime and when their lives are taken. Among other requirements, *kashrut* calls for a near-instantaneous and painless death.

The eco-kosher movement, launched by Rabbi Zalman Schachter-Shalomi[1] in the late 1970s, calls us to include in the definition of kosher a host of other considerations applicable to current times, but rooted in biblical teachings. For example, can we consider an animal kosher if it has been fed grain laced with pesticides? Can factory-farmed chickens be kosher, birds confined to tight quarters and living not on a diurnal cycle but with artificial lighting colored and modulated to increase production?

---

1. Rabbi Zalman Schachter-Shalomi (1924–2014) was the founder and spiritual leader of the Jewish Renewal movement. Reb Zalman, as he was affectionally known, was an educator, mentor, rabbi, spiritual director, and visionary.

Jewish renewal is a worldwide, transdenominational movement grounded in Judaism's prophetic and mystical traditions.

Jewish renewal carries forward Judaism's perpetual process of renewal.

Jewish renewal seeks to bring creativity, relevance, joy, and an all embracing awareness to spiritual practice, as a path to healing our hearts and finding balance and wholeness—tikkun halev.

Taken from the website of ALEPH Alliance for Jewish Renewal: *www.aleph.org*. Used with permission.

Are vegetables acceptable, though neither meat nor dairy, if they've been sprayed with pesticides and grown by exploited farm workers? These are among the questions being addressed by multiple faith traditions.[2]

Eco-kosher concerns are also grounded in a concept probably common to all faith traditions, that of intentionality—in Hebrew, *kavannah*. That is, when we pray or act as part of practicing our faith, we understand that it must be done with willingness and complete honesty, with the desire to do it, and not with a mindset that we are fulfilling an obligation we'd rather not be doing at this time. Thus, if one considers the spirit of the teachings around *kashrut*, it's difficult to accept as kosher, for example, an animal whose owner has shown no "concern for the distress of living creatures." This provides another perspective on the eco-kosher movement. How might the intentionality with which *kashrut* is broadly and generally practiced change the choices we make and the foods we eat? The biblical teachings allow us to eat animals, but not to afflict them in any way while they are being raised, for example, living in cramped quarters, or how their lives are ended, for example, hoisting them upside down while alive by chains wrapped around their ankles.

Factory farming, to take one example, affects more than just the treatment and killing of animals. Most of the animals we eat are produced in factory-like settings, where animals are raised and turned out like so many inanimate objects. We readily grasp that a child raised in appalling physical and psychological conditions might not be as healthy as one raised in appropriate circumstances. Why should we assume something different for animals? And if it's not different, what does that imply about the health of those of us who consume such food?

Award-winning journalist Nicholas Kristof wrote an article featured in the *New York Times* graphically describing the normative, but horrible, methods by which chickens are killed in the U.S. and reporting an Agriculture Department estimate that about 700,000 chickens per year are "not slaughtered correctly" which, as Kristof writes, is "often a euphemism for being scalded to death."[3]

---

2. The Sacred Foods Project is one such coordinated effort; see *www.aleph.org/sacredfoods.htm*.

3. Kristof, Nicholas, "To Kill a Chicken," New York Times, March 15, 2015. *www.nytimes.com/2015/03/15/opinion/sunday/nicholas-kristof-to-kill-a-chicken.html?_r=0*

Our diets include milk, eggs, chicken, beef—numerous foods that constitute the end products of factory farming. *Animal Machines*[4] provides a few examples of small-scale studies that compared the nutritional quality of eggs from factory-raised chickens to free-range chickens. One study reported that the vitamin A and beta-carotene content of factory eggs totaled 4,510 IU per 100 g. For free-range eggs, the two totaled 8,830 IU per 100g, twice the nutritional content. A second study reported that the vitamin B content of free range eggs was also about twice that of factory eggs.

These two findings suggest that we may not be deriving the nutritional value we expect from our food, precisely because of how we raise animals. Americans might benefit from a new and comprehensive inquiry into the nutritional benefits of food from factory-raised animals compared with that from humanely raised, appropriately fed animals. Perhaps consequences of our obsession with low-cost production include the high medical costs incurred to treat a variety of nutritionally based illnesses and, in many cases, shortened lifespans for millions of people.

Are we satisfied with the tradeoff likely carried out by food producers between corporate profits and consumer wellbeing, or would we prefer more healthful food from animals raised appropriately, even if it meant slightly higher prices? If our answer is the latter, then we can accelerate a change by intentionally choosing to purchase meat from animals humanely raised and killed, and asking store managers to make more such products available, particularly in the so-called "food deserts" where quality foods are difficult to find.

Our wellbeing and that of our feed-animals are interrelated. Ultimately, we feel their pain.

---

4. Ruth Harrison, *Animal Machines: The New Factory Farming Industry* (London: Vincent Stuart Ltd., 1964).

DISCUSSION QUESTIONS

1. Why would the right treatment of animals speak so strongly to the early Israelites?

2. How would you react if you learned that there was a difference in nutritional content between factory-raised animals and humanely-raised animals?

3. Discus how we might feed our population without factory farming?

7

Mindfulness and Eating

The rationale for the various dietary laws in the Bible Jesus knew has been a subject of conjecture for centuries. On the surface, however, the laws have the potential to support our connection with the divine, that is, to make us mindful of the divine. This mindfulness differs significantly from the contemporary use of the term, which refers to being fully aware of our own sensations, thoughts, and emotions of the moment.

According to the *Shulchan Aruch*, the Code of Jewish Law,[1] the length of the blade used to slaughter cattle must be at least twice the width of the animal's neck. The blade must be exceedingly sharp to ensure the animal has a fast and painless death, reflecting the "concern for the distress of living creatures." These regulations, part of the laws of *kashrut*, require more in addition: not eating the blood of an animal (Gen. 9:1–4); not consuming a milk product along with meat ("Do not boil a kid in its mother's milk"); and not eating the thigh muscle that is on the socket of the hip (Gen. 32:33, in remembrance of Jacob's hip being wrenched when he wrestled with a being divine and human). Lastly, these laws identify what living beings are acceptable as food and which are prohibited.

Verses 1–23 of the eleventh chapter of Leviticus place constraints upon what land animals, water creatures, birds, and swarming things may be taken as food. Verse 3 states that any animal that has true hooves, with clefts through the hooves, and that chews the cud—such may be eaten. Verses 4–8 identify animals that do one or the other but not both, and thus remain prohibited.

---

1. Shulchan Aruch (Hebrew "Set Table"), Yoreh De'ah 24:2–4 and Mishneh Torah, Sefer Kedusha, Shechitah, chapter 2, Halacha 9 (See *www.chabad.org/library/article_cdo/aid/971828/jewish/Shechitah-Chapter-2.htm*).

Verse 9 opens with, "These you may eat, of all that are in the waters." This permission becomes constrained with the next sentence: Everything in the waters that has fins and scales, whether in the seas or in the streams—such you may eat. Verses 10–11 reinforce this with: "But anything in the seas or the streams that does not have fins and scales, . . . they are detestable to you and detestable they shall remain."

Verses 20–23 deal with "winged insects," identifying those that are an abomination and those that may be eaten. Winged insects that walk on fours are an abomination, except those that have, above their feet, jointed legs to leap with on the ground—these may be eaten; examples of acceptable "winged insects" include the locust, grasshopper, and cricket.

Note that verse 9 opens with "These you may eat, of all that are in the waters," while the next two verses immediately qualify that by identifying what may and may not be eaten. This suggests a literary construct in which the general principle comes first and then the clarifying particulars come later. Sometimes these particulars come in succeeding verses, while other times they occur chapters or books later. Part of our task is to remain attentive and see connections.

This need for connection also occurs with the verse in Genesis 9 that states "Every moving thing that lives shall be food for you; and just as I gave you the green plants, I give you everything," while Leviticus 11 gives a host of qualifying particulars. In fact, scholars used this collective approach with the teaching of "concern for the distress of living creatures," distilled from the collection of verses dealing with obligations to animals.

This finding reinforces the collective approach Part I takes to environmental-related verses in Genesis–Deuteronomy. While Christians and Jews must pay attention to individual verses, we must also strive to discern if they are part of a larger teaching that imparts its own unified instruction.

These passages about living beings permitted and prohibited as food clearly limit our latitude with respect to the natural world from the prevailing interpretation of Genesis 1:28. The Bible does not explain why one animal, fish, or bird may be eaten and others not, but clearly places restrictions. And these constraints involve human-to-nature interactions, not human-to-human behavior.

The commandments that require us to remain mindful of what meat, fowl, and fish we eat reconnect us to the passage in Deuteronomy that begins "Hear, O Israel," "Pay attention, Israel." We pay attention to the covenant—and its sanctions—multiple times a day; by thinking of what we eat, we think of attributes that secure that covenantal relationship. The Bible provides no reasons for these dietary distinctions, and though we might speculate about them, we realize that they require an *attentiveness* to remain faithful to them.

In fact, tradition and linguistic scholarship provide evidence that the commandments are viewed as both actions to perform and a means of joining with God. Arthur Green expresses the word "commandment" (Hebrew, *mitzvah*) as a "sanctified religious deed."[2] Hebrew and Aramaic are cognate languages, meaning that they derive from a common ancestral language. The word *mitzvah* is related to the Aramaic word *tzavta*, meaning to connect or to join. Green writes that the Hasidic tradition[3] interprets the word *mitzvah* to mean "a place of encounter," where the divine and human connect. Thus, the word "commandment" is linked with the words "connect," or "joined together." We can translate *mitzvah* as that which has been *commanded* by God and, equally, as that which *connects* us to God. Thus, following the commandments is one way by which we maintain our connection to God and to the part of creation our actions affect.

In Exodus 23:19 we find the prohibition (stated three times in Genesis–Deuteronomy) that "You shall not boil a kid in its mother's milk." This law speaks only of goats (a kid), but later interpretation extended the prohibition to the mixing of meat and milk of any animal, whether cooked or not; for example, the law prohibits eating a cheeseburger, or a steak with a glass of milk.

A subsequent extension is the practice of using one set of dishes for meals with meat and a second set for non-meat or dairy meals. In Judaism, this is called building a fence around the Torah: instituting practices that ensure that one does not inadvertently violate a commandment.

While the Bible does not provide a reason for forbidding the practice of boiling a kid in its mother's milk, it is noteworthy that the prohibition does not occur in Leviticus 11, which provides most of the dietary regulations. The commentary in *The Torah: A Modern Commentary* advances two theories that have gained credibility over the years. One asserts that the law serves to curb our cruel instincts. In practice, we surmise that one would

---

2. Arthur Green, *Radical Judaism: Rethinking God & Tradition* (New Haven: Yale University Press, 2010,) 97.

3. The Hasidic movement refers to a branch of Orthodox Judaism that arose to emphasize prayer, joy, and religious intensity, rather than the academic study of the sacred texts.

prepare for human consumption a slaughtered baby goat in the milk from the mother that nursed the goat a short while ago. At this time, about three thousand years since it was articulated, the practice carries a triumphalist tone, meant to exemplify humanity's domination over animals. And the practice is forbidden.

A second theory offered by Maimonides (R. Moses ben Maimon, twelfth century) suggests that the prohibition serves as a further attempt to avoid idolatry. His analysis draws on a text describing a Canaanite sacrificial practice that prepares a kid in milk or a lamb in butter. The Canaanites were idol worshippers, and this sacrificial practice was part of an idol-related ritual. The thrice-mentioned prohibition is in line with the emphasis in the Bible of avoiding idolatry.

An additional prohibition was given in Genesis 9:4 which forbids consuming the blood of an animal. This is one of the rare cases when the reason is given: Blood was seen as the life force.

All of the passages cited reveal that our latitude with respect to creation becomes increasingly constrained as we move from Genesis through Deuteronomy—we observe a narrowing of our options. (Recall: "I make this covenant, *with its sanctions*, . . .") Genesis 1:28 does not contain any explicit limitations, but we have now revealed strong constraints building over the intervening books, with many implications. Some of these focus us on the doctrine to exhibit "concern for the distress of living creatures," while others address what may and may not be eaten and what means of preparation may be allowed.

These passages are not listed to suggest they be considered as part of good environmentalism, nor as personal practices, but rather to underline that for those who wish to let the Bible inform their environmental perspective, the text is replete with teachings about the natural world that reveal obligations to remain attentive and compassionate towards that which God created. Attention to these commandments relevant to our faith sustains our connection to the divine.

DISCUSSION QUESTIONS

1. Discuss the connection, if any, between offering a grace before meals and the notion of mindfulness and eating.

2. What do we often express in a grace before meals?

3. Discuss how the offering of a grace before meals might be affected by knowing of the conditions under which the animal was raised.

4. How does it change the experience of a meal when Christians say a blessing before or after meals, and when Jews offer a blessing before eating and a blessing after eating (*Birkat Hamazon*, blessing on nourishment)?

8

Recycling

If one had to select a single practice to symbolize the environmental movement, recycling might be the choice. Reduce, reuse, recycle—we've been hearing that mantra for decades, and individuals, cities, and organizations have embraced it to varying degrees.

The first word in that trilogy—*reduce*—advocates using only what we need for any task, not being wasteful. The second asks that we not discard an item that's been used once if it can be used again. A simple example is a paper towel used to wipe up water; left to dry, it can be used again. Recycle means to convert materials from an item no longer useful into a new object. A familiar example is to use the aluminum of an empty soda can to make a new one, rather than mining bauxite and extracting aluminum in an energy-intensive process.

An early reference to such practices can be found in a twelfth-century commentary on a verse in Deuteronomy. The biblical text reads:

> If you besiege a town for a long time, making war against it in order to take it, you must not destroy its trees by wielding an axe against them. Although you may take food from them, you must not cut them down. Are trees in the field human beings that they should come under siege from you? You may destroy only the trees that you know do not produce food; you may cut them down for use in building siege-works against the town that makes war with you, until it falls.
>
> Deut. 20:19–20

Food-bearing trees—think of olive, date, and fig trees—are not thick and heavy enough to use for defense (siege-works), and therefore cutting them down would simply be punitive and ultimately wasteful, and the Bible prohibits such behavior.

Scholars long ago interpreted this teaching as a prohibition against needless waste, with applications to far more than fruit, olive, and nut trees. The twelfth-century physician and biblical commentator Maimonides summarized an expanded view when he wrote:

> It is not only forbidden to destroy fruit-bearing trees, but whoever breaks vessels, tears clothes, demolishes a building, stops up a fountain or wastes food, in a destructive way, offends against the law of "thou shalt not destroy."[1]

We speak of food, shelter, and clothing as essentials, and this teaching includes all three. The prohibition against needless destruction extends from this interpretation to our most basic needs and is meant to be inclusive. When we choose to turn into trash something that could be reused or recycled, the action violates the instruction "thou shalt not destroy."

The widespread practice of city-wide recycling connects with this biblical teaching, though clearly not instituted for biblical reasons, and is a practice in which we can take pride. It is an important part of reducing greenhouse gas emissions, for making products from recycled materials generally requires less energy than making them from the raw materials. However, recycling should not be one's only activity to slow climate change. We must be far more engaged.

Locations without a municipal recycling program may offer collection points where Individuals can take items such as aluminum, glass, plastic, and paper; for-profit or non-profit businesses then transport and sell the materials to manufacturers who use them as their "raw" material. Recycling leads to less trash in landfills; a slower depletion of natural resources; less air, water, and soil pollution; the growth of new industries; and, in many instances, greater corporate profits.[2]

The website of Interface Global, a large carpet manufacturer, provides one outstanding example of the profitability resulting from reducing waste. Ray Anderson (1934–2011), who led the company and drove the effort to reduce both waste and pollution, became internationally known for his talks on the corporate effort, its achievements, and cost savings. In a 2009 TED

---

1. Louis Jacobs, *The Jewish Religion: A Companion* (Oxford: Oxford University Press, 1995),140.

2. Read about Ray Anderson and the sustainability efforts of the carpet manufacturer Interface: *www.interfaceglobal.com.*

talk,[3] Mr. Anderson said that greenhouse gas (GHG) emissions were down 82 percent in absolute tonnage, fossil fuel use was down by 60 percent, and sales had increased by two-thirds. In 2013, the company's website reported that 36 percent of total energy use was from renewable sources.

The injunction in Deuteronomy against needless waste gets to the heart of the sustainability movement. We practice needless waste when we let vehicles idle unnecessarily, when we waste water, when lights remain on unused, when we choose the disposable product, and in a myriad of other ways. As a society, we might examine the dubious merit of an economic structure that offers a financial incentive for disposing of a product and buying a new one, rather than repairing the existing one. This structure exists, in part, because some of the costs of manufacture and disposal are borne by taxpayers who fund various restoration programs and by governments that permit releasing harmful gases and polluted waste streams that, in some instances, damage our health.

For example, the American Lung Association reports that 138.5 million people live in areas with unhealthful levels of ozone or particle pollutants, or both. Ozone forms when certain gases emitted by tailpipes or smokestacks interact with sunlight. Particle pollution comes from exhaust smoke.

Enforcing existing standards to provide us cleaner air or enacting new, tighter regulations generally raises business operating expenses. Thus, weaker air quality regulations mean lower operating costs, but higher medical expenses. That's the tradeoff we make in many different circumstances.

We use more energy than required to drive our cars; to heat, cool, and light our buildings; and to operate appliances. Our practices are unsustainable, that is, the way we live today assures a diminished quality of life for our children and grandchildren. A 1987 report defined sustainable development as "development that meets the needs of the present without compromising the ability of future generations to meet their needs."[4]

The enormous amount of energy we use, much of it wasted, results in correspondingly huge amounts of greenhouse gases emitted into the atmosphere that, for CO_2, will remain for centuries, and brings about the climate

---

3. TED, which stands for Technology, Entertainment, Design, refers to a set of conferences offered by the non-profit Sapling Foundation. Extraordinary presentations by a wide variety of speakers are available through the Internet at *www. TED.com.*

4. From *Our Common Future*, a report from the 1983 World Commission on Environment and Development conference chaired by Gro Harlem Brundtland, © 1987 United Nations.Reprinted with permission of the United Nations.

change observed. This raises several questions: Do we understand fully the implications of unsustainable? Do we accept the reality of its implications? Do we care? Perhaps that is the most difficult question.

Do we believe that the manifestations of climate change that we have already observed result largely from human activities? The reports of the Intergovernmental Panel on Climate Change (IPCC), a large, diverse group of internationally recognized scientists, provide the most authoritative answer to that question. Their conclusion is that human actions do result in the emission of heat-trapping gases into the atmosphere that bring about: an increase in the earth's average temperature; the melting of Antarctic and Arctic ice sheets; the melting of the Greenland ice sheet; changes in the intensity and frequency of storms; variations in rainfall patterns; changes in agricultural productivity; migrations/reductions/disappearance of species; a rise in sea levels, and a host of other changes. In other words, we are changing the planet into one we have not lived on before.

Some choose to deny the validity of the IPCC scientific conclusions, thus freeing themselves from the responsibility to consider ameliorating measures. Others reject measures that carry a significant price, failing to understand that inaction assures a heavier financial burden in the future, more difficult compensating measures, and more drastic and costly actions to accommodate the inescapable effects of climate change.

In its seventy years, the member countries of the United Nations have not developed the ability to work cooperatively on common environmental objectives. The closest we have come, I believe, is the Montreal Protocol to end emissions of chlorofluorocarbons (CFC) into the atmosphere, gases that destroy the ozone layer and thereby admit damaging levels of ultraviolet-B radiation to the Earth's surface.[5]

---

5. The Montreal Protocol on ozone depleting substances began in 1973 with a finding by Frank Sherwood Roland and Mario Molina that CFC molecules released by a wide variety of spray-can products could result in diminishing the earth's ozone layer, leading to a damaging increase in ultraviolet-B radiation reaching the planet's surface. A 1976 finding by the National Academy of Sciences confirmed the credibility of the ozone depletion hypothesis. A 1985 report from a British Antarctic Survey related observing a surprisingly large hole in the polar ozone layer. Nevertheless, for thirteen years the leaders of certain chemical and spray-can companies vigorously disputed that a problem existed, even after the 1985 publication of confirmed findings. The Montreal Protocol of 1987 constitutes perhaps the second most important international agreement affecting our environment. As of September 2009, all UN countries have ratified the original Montreal Protocol. (*www.unep.org*) First place in UN environmental accords now belong, I believe, to the agreement on greenhouse gas reductions signed by 196 nations in December 2015. (*http://the guardian.com/environment/2015/dec/13/paris-climate-deal-cop-diplomacy-developing-united-nations*)

The agreement prevented devastating consequences for human, animal, and plant life on this planet and is achieving the desired result. The ozone layer is starting to recover, according to a panel of three hundred scientists that reports on this topic to the United Nations.[6] It will take, however, until 2050 for the mid-latitude ozone layer to return to healthy 1980 conditions and until 2075 for the layer over the Antarctic to recover. We need to remain mindful of that two-generation period for repair (1987–2050), and look into the eyes of children as we debate and postpone world-wide climate mitigation efforts. Nature heals slowly.

Part of what the leaders of each country must determine is how to equalize the adjustments necessary among the nations and then, in our case, sell those particular measures to congresspersons with one or two years until reelection and senators with one to six years left until reelection. More challenging still is obtaining cooperation from our vast and powerful corporate sector, whose time horizon is the quarterly report.[7]

While it might seem questionable that individual actions can appreciably affect a planet-wide problem, a critical mass of people can create an atmosphere receptive to measures that will alleviate the effects of climate change.

One contribution toward that receptivity lies in understanding that centuries of biblical interpretation that God has given us the earth to master and rule as we wish is likely an incorrect reading of the text. We saw this vividly in the Noah section, both in Genesis 7 and in Genesis 9. Rather, the Bible that Christians and Jews hold sacred places numerous limitations upon our behavior toward the natural world, meaning that we have been treating the environment in ways that damage our personal relationship to the divine. Christians and Jews who care about that relationship may seek to change personal behavior and find motivation to influence national policies.

I would argue that this does not mean advocating the enactment of public policies based on religious teachings. A necessary condition for any shift in policy is compelling evidence that change is needed. Only at the point when the evidence is in (with climate change, I believe that it is) and experts have provided recommendations on the actions required (rarely

---

6. Gail Sullivan, "Earth's ozone layer is recovering," *Washington Post*, September 11, 2014, *http://www.washingtonpost.com/news/morning-mix/wp/2014/09/11/try-to-keep-up-earths-ozone-layer-is-recovering-but-that-is-making-global-warming-worse/*.

7. A compelling point the author heard from Vice President Al Gore at the American Institute of Architects 2007 national convention.

unanimous, of course, but addressed in Part II) do we make our individual decisions, influenced by the evidence and, in part, by forces of which we may be only barely aware: our upbringing, education, life experiences, and religious beliefs.

The last sentence in Deuteronomy 20:19, the teaching with which we began this section, connects poignantly with a verse in Genesis 9: "Are trees in the field human beings that they should come under siege from you?" That is, human beings finding themselves under siege while outside a city can flee into the city for protection. Trees, along with other parts of the natural world, cannot escape the destructive forces, leading to the fear and the dread predicted in Genesis 9. Recall the verse after the flood: "The fear and dread of you shall rest on every animal of the earth, and on every bird of the air, on everything that creeps on the ground, and on all the fish of the sea; into your hand they are delivered." Our shaping and forming the world has included destructive actions that nature cannot evade.

In shaping the world, we have ignored the most obvious extrapolations of biblical commandments, in part because it has been convenient to do so and in part because Christianity effectively replaced the Old Testament with the New Testament (NT) and thereby lost touch with its foundational teachings. That is, over the centuries, Christians chose not to maintain roughly equal contact with the Old Testament and the New Testament, but steadily elevated the NT as the primary reference and reduced contact with the Bible of Jesus and the writers of the Gospels.

At the beginning of this third millennium, Americans must add chemicals to water to destroy the contaminants we have added; must breathe air we have polluted; consume food with residues of insecticides and antibiotics given to animals who contract diseases because of how we raise them; and battle or succumb to diseases, many traceable to an unhealthful environment and food supply. We can do better.

DISCUSSION QUESTIONS

1. Maimonides expanded the teaching in Deuteronomy 20:19 against cutting down food-bearing trees to include not breaking vessels, demolishing buildings, or tearing clothes. How does this apply to our lives today?

2. Discuss your thoughts about recycling, given its roots in Deuteronomy and the teaching of Maimonides.

3. Discuss your personal efforts to avoid being wasteful.

9

The Land

The ancient Israelites were not wrestling with issues such as storing radioactive nuclear fuel or coping with mercury from electricity power plants when they extracted biblical teachings concerning treatment of the land. But even these modern dilemmas are covered under a principle the Pentateuch—those first five books—yields.

A man asked the great scholar Hillel[1] to teach him Torah while he stood on one foot. Hillel replied, "What is hateful to you, do not to your neighbour; that is the whole Torah, while the rest is the commentary thereof; go and learn it."[2] That synthesis by Hillel was also given by Jesus in its positive form: "In everything do to others as you would have them do to you; for this is the law and the prophets." (Matt. 7:12) This provides a powerful principle by which to measure the appropriateness, relative to the Bible, of human-to-human interaction. We seek a synthesis, comparable in brevity, for human-to-nature interaction.

For development and economic reasons, among others, it has been profoundly convenient to be guided primarily by

> "Be fruitful and multiply, and fill the earth and subdue it; and have dominion over the fish of the sea and over the birds of the air and over every living thing that moves upon the earth"
>
> Gen. 1:28

rather than to consider the numerous commandments elsewhere in Genesis–Deuteronomy that constrain our actions.

---

1. Hillel was born in Babylon and lived in Jerusalem during the period of King Herod. He died around 10–20 CE

2. *Babylonian Talmud*, tractate Shabbath 31a, Soncino Edition, 532.

Our previous chapters were organized in terms of contemporary environmental issues: maintaining biological diversity; recycling, or not destroying what still has use; the treatment of animals and its connection to farming and fishing. Each chapter has cited and synthesized the central teachings relating to each category.

When first-century scholars looked into the vast number of biblical verses relating to agriculture, they found that they could be grouped into ten distinct categories[3]—once again a collective approach. The ten categories are Peah (Corner), Demai (Doubtful produce), Kilaim (Of two sorts), Sheviit (Seventh year), Terumot (Donations), Maaserot (Tithes), Maaser Sheni (Second tithe), Hallah (Chunk of dough), Orlah (Restrictions (with trees)), Bikkurim (First fruits). These categories organize the effects of the commandments on the actions of the biblical Israelites, and offer us a lens to guide our actions with respect to the land.

The ten categories of practices and the multiple instructions within each are rooted in the belief that the land God gave to the Israelites for their use remains the possession of God:

> The land shall not be sold in perpetuity, for the land is mine; with me you are but aliens and tenants.

> Lev. 25:23

The term "Holy Land" may derive from this one verse.

The geographic boundaries of the land God gave the Israelites to use are described in several places, including Numbers 34:1–12 and Genesis 15:18–21. Each of these descriptions is slightly different from the others, leaving biblical scholars to either address the differences or deduce arguments for their commonality.

Eight of these categories do not relate to a modern discussion because they either involve the Second Temple (destroyed in 70 CE), its priests, and the Levites, or apply directly to the land that the Torah states God gave to the Israelites.

Instructions involving the first of the eight categories concern tithing part of the crops to the temple priests and the Levites, offering of first fruits, and restrictions for three years on the yield of all kinds of trees for food. The temple no longer exists, nor its priests, though tithing remains a practice in many faith traditions.

---

3. The ten categories are found in ten sections of Zeraim (Seeds), one of the sections of the Talmud.

Instructions involving the second group in the eight categories comprise rules about the Sabbatical year: When the Israelites entered the land God gave them, they could work the fields for six years, but the seventh year was to be one of rest for the land. They were neither to plant nor to work their fields or their orchards. They could eat what the land produced, but not work the fields.

One may view the Sabbatical year as an analog of the fourth of the Ten Commandments, the one concerning the Sabbath. That is, the household and cattle of biblical Israelites lived on a diurnal cycle, and were instructed not to work on the seventh cycle, the seventh day. However, the cycle for the land may be viewed as a year, the time it takes to pass through the four seasons. The land also was to rest on the seventh cycle, the seventh year.

The instructions about the Sabbatical year remind us of the pull between the biblically designated land and the entire earth. That is, in Leviticus 25:23 with commandments about the Jubilee year, we find, "for the land is mine," with "the land" presumably referring to the area designated in Numbers 34.

In accord with this, Alan Avery-Peck provided an overarching perspective on these ten categories when he wrote, "The same notion of God's ownership of the land explains Scripture's insistence that the land be used only in ways commensurate with the holiness of its owner."[4]

That is, if we look at the collection of teachings in Genesis–Deuteronomy that relate to the land given to the Israelites, we find that they convey the broad instruction that one must use the land and consume its crops in a manner reflecting its ownership by God.

Consider this perspective and the practice of blasting the tops off mountains to access coal. This violent, abusive treatment of the land violates Avery-Peck's synthesis and is just one example of a misuse of the land that contributes to greenhouse gas emissions.

The fact that the Bible instructs us to acknowledge God's ownership of the land further questions Lynn White's reading of the Bible that "no item in the physical creation had any purpose save to serve man's purposes." Rather, the Bible establishes a covenantal relationship between God and all life on earth (recall the first covenant), with special obligations falling upon

---

4. Alan J. Avery-Peck, *Mishnah's Division of Agriculture: A History and Theology of* Seder Zeraim (Chico, CA: Scholars Press, 1985), xiii.

humans.[5] When the Bible calls us to rest on the seventh day, and to let the land rest every seven years, it does so explicitly in remembrance of creation, not only for our betterment—which depends on the wellbeing of the land.

The tug between the particular and the universal comes clearly into view with the opening of the familiar Psalm 24, which shifts us to a global perspective:

> The earth is the LORD's and all that is in it, the world, and those who live in it.

Thus God's dominion extends everywhere. That is also the view at the revelation at Sinai when God says: "Indeed, the whole earth is mine." (Exod. 19:5) That viewpoint also appears in 1 Kings 8:27, when Solomon speaks at the dedication of the temple:

> But will God indeed dwell on the earth? Even heaven and the highest heaven cannot contain you, much less this house that I have built!

The question of applicability arises throughout the Bible. Observant Jews view the laws identifying what we may and may not eat as applying to them wherever they reside. Similarly, Jews assume the collection of teachings that gave rise to the doctrine of "concern for the distress of living creatures" applies wherever they live, not just to scriptural adherents in the Holy Land.

Therefore, while parts of the Bible point to a specific piece of geography, the Psalms, later writings, and parts of Torah explicitly adopt a global perspective. It is that global perspective of the Bible's teachings on the environment that we seek now.

One of the two categories that remain, returning to the principle referred to earlier, concerns the inseparability between use of the land and obligations to the needy. Two of the biblical passages that convey this perspective are:

> When you reap the harvest of your land, you shall not reap to the very edges of your field, or gather the gleanings of your harvest. You shall not

---

5. We might posit that these special obligations fall upon us because we, alone, are created in the image of God: "So God created humankind in his image, in the image of God he created them; male and female he created them." (Gen. 1:27)

strip your vineyard bare, or gather the fallen grapes of your vineyard; you shall leave them for the poor and the alien: I am the LORD your God.

Lev. 19:9–10

When you reap your harvest in your field and forget a sheaf in the field, you shall not go back to get it; it shall be left for the alien, the orphan, and the widow, so that the LORD your God may bless you in all your undertakings. When you beat your olive trees, do not strip what is left; it shall be for the alien, the orphan, and the widow.

When you gather the grapes of your vineyard, do not glean what is left; it shall be for the alien, the orphan, and the widow. Remember that you were a slave in the land of Egypt; therefore I am commanding you to do this.

Deut. 24:19–22

As the ancient Israelites harvested crops from the land they had worked, we understand that they did not collect the yield from the very boundaries of the land, but left that for the hungry. Similarly, they did not gather what had fallen during the harvest, the gleanings, nor did they repeatedly shake or beat trees seeking to increase the yield from them. What remained on the trees and on the vines, and what lay on the ground and at the edges of the fields, were for those in need. We find scriptural confirmation of the practice of gleaning in the book of Ruth:[6]

She [Ruth] came and gleaned in the field behind the reapers. As it happened, she came to the part of the field belonging to Boaz, who was of the family of Elimelech.

Ruth 2:3

Ruth and her mother-in-law, Naomi, were in the land of Judah, having come from Moab, and had no way to provide for themselves.

When we now give to those who are hungry, we may contribute to a food bank or send a check to a charitable organization. That is, we transfer some of what we have to others. In the above verses from Leviticus and Deuteronomy, the one who works the land does not take possession of the produce intended for the needy. The food remains on the ground or on the trees, acknowledging that what comes forth from God's earth belongs to

---

6. Ruth, 2:3, 2:17, 2:23.

God and must be divided between the landowner and the needy in a prescribed manner.

The distances between most farms and the cities where many in need reside now preclude this means of food distribution. However, keeping in mind these biblical teachings about God's ownership of what the land yields can enhance our connection to the divine each time we help those who are hungry.

These regulations for the ancient Israelites helped maintain an awareness between enjoying the earth's produce and the needs of the less fortunate. By harvesting in a way that provided food for those in need, they believed they were helping to sustain their connection to God. The message for us is that it's not take, take, take, but take and provide, take and provide. In twenty-first century terms, those who "harvest" a good living have a biblical obligation to help provide sustenance to the hungry. Or, put another way, God stipulates that we may enjoy the bounty of God's earth as long as we attend to those in need.

To a degree, we have extended this practice into modern times and benefit, if mindful, in a similar way. Many cities and towns collect food for the poor. Some places operate food banks that distribute donated food. Other places have storehouses to which those who are hungry may come and obtain food. In far too many places, regrettably, the hungry engage in "dumpster-diving" or the equivalent to find food, and in many locations Americans go hungry. In a land of plenty, we have no excuse for permitting this.

These Leviticus passages can be manifested in the twenty-first century by ensuring that whenever we purchase food for ourselves, we also purchase some for those in need—evidence of need is abundant,[7] and by creating and maintaining an infrastructure that connects the donated food to those who need it.

As we give food out of each trip to the grocery store, we also benefit by remaining mindful of why we do this: fulfilling this obligation helps connect us to the divine. It is one instance of that sweeping covenantal statement,

> If you follow my statutes and keep my commandments and observe them
> faithfully, I will give you your rains in their season, and the land shall yield

---

7. In 2013, 17.5 million U.S. households were food insecure. In that same year, 45.3 million people were in poverty, and 19.9 million Americans lived in extreme poverty. Source: World Hunger Education Service: *www.worldhunger.org.*

its produce, and the trees of the field shall yield their fruit. . . . And I will walk among you, and will be your God, and you shall be my people.

Lev. 26:3–12

Just as acting responsibly and constraining a child from playing in the street can avoid a tragedy that severs the bond between parent and child, so personally accepting biblical constraints with regard to creation can avoid severing the bond that tethers us to the divine. With the divine, we have the capability of restoring the connection, though with the first instance we do not.

The second practice to which attention remains relevant in contemporary times is the prohibition against sowing a field with two different kinds of seeds or wearing clothes of wool and linen. One biblical passage from which this restriction originates is:

You shall not sow your vineyard with a second kind of seed, or the whole yield will have to be forfeited, both the crop that you have sown and the yield of the vineyard itself.

You shall not plough with an ox and a donkey yoked together. You shall not wear clothes made of wool and linen woven together.

Deut. 22:9–11 (See also Lev. 19:19)

As with many of the biblical commandments, no reasons are given for these prohibitions. Scholars noted, however, that since wool comes from an animal while linen comes from a plant, the commandments have the effect of maintaining the distinctions between species.[8] Similarly, by not sowing a field with two different kinds of seeds, we maintain the distinctions between crops. Whether or not one chooses to follow these practices, it is clear that they represent further constraints upon our actions towards the natural world.

Recall that Genesis 7 addresses our modern concern of preserving biological diversity. With these passages from Leviticus and Deuteronomy, we find constraints applicable to agricultural practices that serve, in part, to maintain diversity.

Genetic engineering presents a modern practice that confronts this head-on. Producing a tomato with the gene of a fish not only loses the

---

8. Rachel Adler, *Engendering Judaism: An Inclusive Theology and Ethics* (Philadelphia: The Jewish Publication Society, 1998), 127.

distinctions between species, but represents an outcome not possible by natural means. This is not an extension of grafting, but a fundamentally different process.

Whether or not one acknowledges a religious issue with genetic engineering, and the debate is on, I suggest that there exists a compelling practical one. Introducing such manufactured crops into our food supply means consumers serve as laboratory animals: while we may have short-term findings that indicate no significant difference between the natural food and the genetically modified one, it will take generations of humans before we can identify the side effects and draw conclusions about safety. And this presupposes that we look for them! I concur with Neil Postman, who characterized our society as a "technopoly," a term that designates "the submission of all forms of cultural life to the sovereignty of technique and technology."[9]

In this application of the Deuteronomy and Leviticus prohibitions against mixtures (Lev. 19:19), each individual can decide about consuming genetically modified foods and perhaps, by extension, about organic and conventional products. To enable that personal decision requires our government to enforce labeling that makes such decisions possible. I suggest that we strenuously advocate for this, although succeeding is difficult in a technopoly.[10]

Thus far in this chapter, we've discovered that interactions with the land reveal biblical teachings that tie use of the land to care for those in need, and prohibit planting seeds of two different types in the same field. These teachings illustrate additional ways in which our latitude with respect to the natural world is far narrower than what we infer from Genesis 1:28. But these instructions engender a mindfulness, an awareness that serves to tether us to the divine, and as a result both the adherent and the earth benefit abundantly.

Let us now turn to unhappy prospects of drought, attacks by wild beasts, pestilence, and exile. Such are some of the consequences, listed in Leviticus 26:14–46, that the Israelites would face if they failed to adhere to the regulations of the covenant, particularly to let the land rest on sabbatical

---

9. Neil Postman, *Technopoly: The Surrender of Culture to Technology* (New York: Alfred A. Knopf, 1992), 52.

10. One could make the argument that not labeling genetically modified (GM) foods prevents the practice of one's religion. This has become an issue for observant Jews with the possible introduction of GM salmon that contains genetic material from an eel—a prohibited food.

years. One conclusion from this lengthy passage is that the Bible places great importance on using the land in ways that are "commensurate with the holiness of its owner."[11]

Many scholars view the teaching to let the land rest on sabbatical years as only applying within the Holy Land. Some may wish to take a global perspective, given the Exodus 19:5 assertion that, "Indeed, the whole earth is mine." In that case, this would appear to offer a significant challenge to huge farms with many employees. However, for those wishing to follow this teaching, perhaps a combination of the following would make this feasible: (1) letting a different one-seventh of the land rest every year would put one in compliance with the spirit, if not the letter, of the teaching. The familiar practice of crop rotation and letting a portion of a field lie fallow clearly harmonize with this idea and the sabbatical year generally; and (2) a Sabbatical Year Bank (funded by cooperating farmers) that provided financial support to farmers who observed this, if help were needed.

Leviticus 26:14–46 exemplifies verses cited by some as evidence of the harshness of God as portrayed in the Old Testament, the harshness both of the language used and the punishments listed. From my perspective this is an incorrect reading, and one worth exploring.

We can address the harshness by observing that Leviticus 26:14 explicitly references breaking the covenant.

> But if you will not obey me, and do not observe all these commandments,
> if you spurn my statutes, and abhor my ordinances, so that you will not
> observe all my commandments, and you break my covenant, I in turn will
> do this to you.
>
> Lev. 26:14–16

It should not seem surprising that breaking the covenant with God would have consequences. However, throughout the extended narrative we find multiple places where the description of consequences pauses and allows us time to return to compliance before a harsher consequence is described. "And if . . . you will not obey me . . ." "If you continue hostile to me . . ." (Lev. 26:14–33). That is, only if we do not return to the covenant within some unspecified period of time do other consequences follow.

---

11. Avery-Peck, *Mishnah's Division of Agriculture*, xiii.

This option of returning to a covenantal relationship is a central concept of Judaism, called *t'shuvah*—a turning or return. This is what Jews are asked to do on the Day of Atonement. When the Second Temple stood, the people carried out specific rituals and the high priest made expiation for their sins. With the temple gone, it is now up to individuals to repent: to express remorse for transgressions, to repair or compensate for the damages, and to declare one's intent not to repeat them. In that case, forgiveness is assured. That is, a sincere and complete expression of repentance brings forgiveness.

The multiple pauses in the Leviticus 26 passage signal that God desires our turning, that judgment is not immediate. Thus, any suggestion of harshness must be seen in the light of continuing opportunities to return. Jews see a God of patience and compassion. Moreover, the section concludes with the reminder that God will not break the covenant with the people:

> Yet for all that, when they are in the land of their enemies, I will not spurn them, or abhor them so as to destroy them utterly and break my covenant with them; for I am the LORD their God;

Lev. 26:44

A similar list of potential harsh consequences occurs in Deuteronomy 11:16–21 that Jews include in the daily liturgy following the *Shema* prayer: "Hear, O Israel; the Lord is our God, the Lord is One." The verse from Deuteronomy opens with "Take care, or you will be seduced into turning away, serving other gods and worshipping them."

It is not hard to make the case that what many in the developed world worship is money, making it another god. People with means have great influence including, if they wish, the ability to attain positions of political power and then, even more strongly, to shape the societies in which they live. For many, money is the measure of success.

The perspective on our agricultural production practices has changed to the *societal* teaching that the goal is to *maximize* profit, which can come at the expense of the land, people, and animals. Our practices did not derive from goals such as:

- Producing the most nutritious food possible;
- Ensuring the food is free from substances that could possibly harm the body;

- Raising cattle with the understanding that they are sentient beings that feel both pain and affection and whose physical and mental wellbeing are ultimately reflected in their bodies and, consequently, in what we consume.

We could add to this list: using the land in a way that ensures care for the needy. "In everything do to others as you would have them do to you." (Matt. 7:12)

We live at a point in time when the world population is increasing and weather effects are imposing a heightened unpredictability on the food supply:

> Drought and high temperatures during the 2012 growing season affected many agricultural regions in the United States. For the third consecutive year, national average corn yields were below trend expectations due to weather. Similarly, weather pushed national average soybean yields below trend for the second year in a row. As a result, there is a renewed interest in the relationship between weather and yields for these crops.[12]

Quite obviously, there is a high correlation between weather and food production. Climate change will not just bring warmer temperatures and melting ice caps but, among other effects, increased fluctuation in the food available and a potential rise in food costs.

In recent years, we have endured bouts of prolonged droughts and torrential rains, both of which decrease what the land can produce. We ignore this at our peril. It may be that many of those now in positions of power feel no obligation to avert this disaster, realizing that they will not be living at the time the pain becomes acute. Those who do care for future generations, though conscious of mortality, have an obligation to act.

A diminishing capacity to reliably feed ourselves may result, ultimately, from climate change and its causes: air pollution in the form of CO_2 and other gases that enter the atmosphere. As air pollution did exist in biblical times, we will examine in a later chapter the teachings ancient scholars developed to address it. This will bring biblical teachings directly to bear on the central environmental problem of our time.

---

12. Part of the introduction to *Weather Effects on Expected Corn and Soybean Yields*, Paul C. Westcott and Michael Jewison, Economic Research Service, USDA, FDS-13g-01, July 2013.

DISCUSSION QUESTIONS

1. Discuss the verse in Leviticus that states, ". . . the land is mine; with me you are but aliens and tenants."

2. Discuss Avery-Peck's teaching that ". . . the land be used only in ways commensurate with the holiness of its owner."

3. Discuss the linkage between use of the land and care of the needy.

4. Are prohibitions against mixtures relevant in our lives today?

5. Consider Lev. 26:14–46 and whether you agree with the author's interpretation of multiple options to change, or return. Does this affect your perception of God as depicted in Genesis–Deuteronomy?

10

Care of Creation

The introduction to this book opened with the words of Jesus from the Sermon on the Mount, as given in the Gospels of Matthew and Luke: he came to fulfill the law and the Prophets, the law given in the books Genesis–Deuteronomy.

The previous chapters have demonstrated that our inattention to creation care violates huge swaths of the Law of which Jesus spoke. The Law calls us to preserve all species and defines our relationship with them throughout its five books, yet our fossil fuel emissions are causing species extinctions at an alarming rate and bringing intense distress to many others—including ourselves—through tornados, fires, heat waves, droughts, and storms.

The law teaches us not to destroy food-bearing trees even in time of war, yet through drought, fire, and clear-cutting we destroy forest after forest of food-bearing and other life-giving trees.

The law teaches that the land belongs to God and that its use must be commensurate with the holiness of its owner. Yet through droughts, fires, deluges, erosion, and increases in insect populations we turn huge portions of the land to wasteland (at least temporarily) and, in the process, reduce our food supply.

The law instructs us to observe the Sabbath in remembrance of the work of creation and the day of rest that followed. Yet humans dishonor the created world we inherited, and many ignore the Sabbath as well—which God revealed to Moses on Mt. Sinai as a sign of a covenant.[1]

These and other practices that ignore biblical instructions and damage creation weaken our connection to the divine. What does it say of a

---

1. Exodus 31:16–17

people who professes its faith in houses of worship and knowingly violates the tenets of that faith outside those sanctuaries? And what does it say of clergy who do not call for accountability?

We know that the proverbial frog in water steadily being heated will perish. We move in an atmosphere that is steadily being heated. Aware of both a looming environmental disaster and of biblical violations, we imperil our survival and our connection to God.

We would do well to question our intelligence and our piety.

It is past time to turn our attention to the environmental evidence and biblical teachings, and to dismiss the venal propaganda of those speaking from short-term self-interest. People who knowingly disregard even the wellbeing of their own children do not merit our attention. Those with a moral vision must bring power to bear against the power of the "immoral society" in order to preserve the hospitable world we inherited.

Consider this: What we know is true we also believe is true, but what we believe is true we don't yet know to be true. We usually understand the difference between belief and knowledge, but this pesky distinction can call for our attention at surprising moments. For example, our review of Genesis–Deuteronomy has sought to discern as best we can how the Bible instructs Christians and Jews to act, to continually compare our individual and collective actions against that standard as understood now, and to make changes when appropriate.

And one does that knowing that there is a difference between belief and knowledge. That is, if I release a pen from my hand, I know it will fall to the floor. I do not know the will of God with equal certainty. Some speak of God as all-knowing, all-powerful, and readily agree that they are not. Yet some maintain, with absolute certainty, that they know what they (and others) must do to fulfill God's wishes. Remaining aware of the distinction between belief and knowledge enables us to engage in biblical interpretation with both openness and humility.

Part I of this book includes teachings from numerous biblical passages, yet I realize that there exists an inherent uncertainty in the foundational text, the Torah, with its lack of vowels and punctuation, as described earlier, and understand that the instructions derived from verses today may or may not be in complete harmony with the intent of those teachings written down over 2,200 years ago. The numerous volumes of the Talmud (discussed below) and successive commentaries offer disciplined interpretative responses to much of that uncertainty, but not to all. We strive to understand each verse, and collectively they form a foundation for our set of beliefs. But our common expression, "religious beliefs," conveys that our level of certainty is less than that for the laws of physics.

The next section refers to one of the books of the Talmud, requiring some explanation of this enormous body of work.

For years prior to and after the destruction of the Second Temple in 70 CE,[2] scholars worked to understand the precise meanings of the instructions found in the Torah and to resolve the questions that arose about their implementation in communities. These deliberations and decisions, passed on orally, grew into an increasingly large body of regulations. Eventually, rabbinic scholars began to write down this oral law. Their writings were collected and edited by Rabbi Yehuda Hanasi, who died about 220 CE, into a text called the Mishnah. There are six major sections in the Mishnah, each of which contains between seven and twelve tractates, or books.

After its completion, rabbinic scholars began to write commentaries on the Mishnah that were eventually compiled into a companion text called the Gemara. The primary part of what Jews call the Talmud consists of the Mishnah and Gemara.

Two versions of the Talmud exist, one written in the Land of Israel and completed around 400 CE, called the Jerusalem Talmud, and one compiled in Babylon completed about 600 CE, called the Babylonian Talmud (BT). The Mishnah is similar in both versions, while the Gemara differs. In standard printing, the Babylonian Talmud is about 10,000 pages long.

A page of Talmud appears quite confusing, for it contains not only a section of the Mishnah and the accompanying passages from the Gemara, but at least seven other commentaries written in the four margins that further explain the text. Figures 4 and 5 display a page of the Talmud in English and Hebrew.[3]

The crowded pages of the Talmud provide a snapshot in time of the *ongoing* striving "with beings divine and human" (Gen. 32:28) that Waskow termed our enterprise of God-wrestling.

The concluding chapter of Part I, "Beyond Deuteronomy," looks at regulations in one book of the Talmud that connect with OT and NT teachings.

---

2. The First Temple was built during the reign of King Solomon, 970–931 BCE. The Second Temple period was from 516 BCE to 70 CE, the year it was destroyed by the Romans.

3. *www.joshua-parker.net/portfolio/resourceguides/talmud_layout.pdf.* Used with permission.

A Guide to the Layout of a Talmud Page

PAGE   TRACTATE NAME   CHAPTER NUMBER   CHAPTER NAME

[6] **EIN MISH-PAT, NER MITZVAH:** (Heb., 'Well of Justice, Lamp of Commandment') Two indices compiled by R' Yehoshua Boaz in the sixteenth century. These provide references to major Jewish law codes that report authoritative rulings on topics covered in the Mishnah and Gemara. External works referenced in this way include Rambam's (12th c., Spain and Egypt) *Mishneh Torah* (Heb., Repition of the Law'), the *Shulkhan Arukh* (Heb., 'Set Table') of R' Yosef b. Ephraim Caro (16th c., Israel), the *Arba'ah Turim* (Heb., 'Four Rows') of R' Ya'akov b. Asher (14th c. Spain), and the *Sefer Mitzvot Gadol* (Heb., 'Great Book of Commandments' of R' Moshe b. Ya'akov of Coucy (13th c, France).

[9] **OTHER COMMENTARIES:** Various other commentaries appear in the margins of a printed page of Talmud. None of these minor works cover the entire Talmud,

[4] **TOSAFOT:** *The Tosafot (Heb., 'additions') are medieval commentaries on the text of the Talmud composed mainly in the twelfth and thirteenth centuries. The Tosafot are not the product of a single author or school of commentators, but are rather the work of a variety of talmudic scholars living mainly in France, Germany, and Spain. While Rashi's comments focus on the plain meaning of the text, the tosafists tend to concentrate on analysis of difficult passages, exploring issues, contradictions, and problems raised by the text of the Gemara. Often the Tosafot approach a subject using the logic and style of inquiry of the Gemara. Occasionally Tosefot address an interpretation or explaination offered by Rashi to examine it more thoroughly or to present an alternative approach to the subject. On a printed Talmud page, the comments of the Tosefot are set in a semi-cur-*

[1] **MISHNAH:** The Mishnah (Heb., 'repetition') is the primary record of the teaching, decisions, and disputes of a group of Jewish religious and judicial scholars, known as *Tannaim*, who were active from about 30 BCE to 200 CE, mostly in the areas now known as Israel and Palestine. Originally transmitted orally, the Mishnah was redacted into its current form and committed to writing around the year 200 CE by R' Yehudah haNasi. The language of the Mishnah is Hebrew. The Mishnah is divided into sixty-three 'tractates,' which are organized into six 'orders' according to their subject matter.

[2] **GEMARA:** The Gemara (Aramaic, 'study,') is an analysis of and expansion upon the material presented in the Mishnah. Taken together, the Mishnah and Gemara make up the Talmud. The Gemara records the oral discussions of a group of scholars, known as *Amoraim*, who were active from about 200 to 500 CE, in the areas of present day Iraq, Israel, and Palestine. These discussions often center around statements of the *Tannaim* and are structured by the anonymous voice of a redactor (or group of redactors) known as the *stam* (Heb., 'plain' or 'unattributed'). There are two versions of the Gemara. The *Yerushalmi* (also known as the 'Jerusalem' or 'Palestinian' Talmud) was compiled in what is now northern Israel around 400 CE. The *Bavli* or Babylonian Talmud was redacted about a hundred years later in the Jewish communities of Mesopotamia. Traditionally the redaction of the *Bavli* is attributed to R' Ashi and his student Ravina. The *Talmud Bavli* is the more commonly studied of the two and is considered to be more authoritative when the two offer different legal rulings. The primary language of the Gemara in both versions is Aramaic, although quoted material in Hebrew is common (mostly from biblical texts or earlier *tannaic* material), and words in Greek, Latin, or other languages occasionally occur. In literary form, the Gemara is a complex combination of legal debate, case law, legend, textual analysis, and philosophical inquiry. Its subject matter covers nearly every imaginable facet of ancient Jewish life, ranging from religious, civil, and criminal law to biblical interpretation to speculation about and investigation of the natural world.

[3] **RASHI:** *Rashi (an acronym for R' Shlomo Yitzchaki) was an eleventh century scholar active in France. Rashi compiled the first complete commentary on the Talmud. His commentary focuses on helping students understand the plain meaning of the text. Both the Mishnah and Gemara are written in a brief, terse style, without the use of punctuation or vowel markings. Rashi's comments are therefore directed toward helping readers work their way through the text and understand its basic form and content. Rashi also offers explanations of unusual or rare vocabulary and concepts and occasionally indicates preferred readings in cases where manuscripts differ. Rashi's commentary is always set in a semi-cursive typeface called 'Rashi script,' is positioned on the gutter side of a printed page of Talmud.*

[7] **TORAH OR:** (Heb., 'Torah is Light') Compiled by R' Yehoshua Boaz (16th c., Italy), this index provides citations for biblical references.

[5] **MESORET HASHAS:** (Heb., 'Transmission of the Six Orders') An index compiled by R' Yehoshua Boaz (16th c. Italy), later expanded by R' Yesheyahu Berlin (18th c., Germany), *Mesoret haShas* provides cross references to similar passages elsewhere in the Talmud.

[8] **GLOSSES:** Most modern printed Talmud editions include short definitions, comments, emendations, and cross references from a variety of scholars active during the 17th through 19th centuries. Among the most important of these commentaries are those of R' Eliyahu b. Shlomo (the 'Gra,' or 'Gaon of Vilna,' 18th c., Lithuania), the *Hagahot haBah* (Heb.: 'Commentaries of the Bah') of R' Yoel Sirkes (17th c., Poland), the comments of R' Yesheyahu Berlin (18th c., Germany), and the *Gilyon haShas* (Heb.: 'Marginalia on the Six Orders') of R' Akiva Eger (19th c., Germany).

sive typeface known as 'Rashi script,' and they always appear immediately adjacent to the Mishnah and Gemara in the large block of text positioned opposite Rashi's commentary.

so different tractates include different commentaries in this area. Among these are the comments of Rabbenu Chananel (11th c., Tunisia), the *Sefer haMafteah* (Heb., 'Book of the Key') of R' Nissin (11th c., Tunisia), *Tosefot Yeshanim* (Heb.: 'Additions of the Ancients') 13th c. France and Germany), the *Mainz Commentary* compiled by the students of Rabbenu Gershom b. Yehudah (11th c., Germany), the *Tosefot Rid* (Heb.: 'Additions of the Rid') of R' Yesheyahu diTrani (13th c., Italy), and the *Shittah Mequbbetzet* (Heb: 'Gathered Interpretation') of R' Bezalel Ashkenazi (16th c., Egypt and Jerusalem).

Figure 4

A Guide to the Layout of a Talmud Page

[1] Mishnah

[2] Gemara

[3] Rashi's Commentary

[4] Tosefot

[5] Mesoret haShas

[6] Ein Mishpat, Ner Mitzvah

[7] Torah Or

[8] Glosses

[9] Other Commentaries

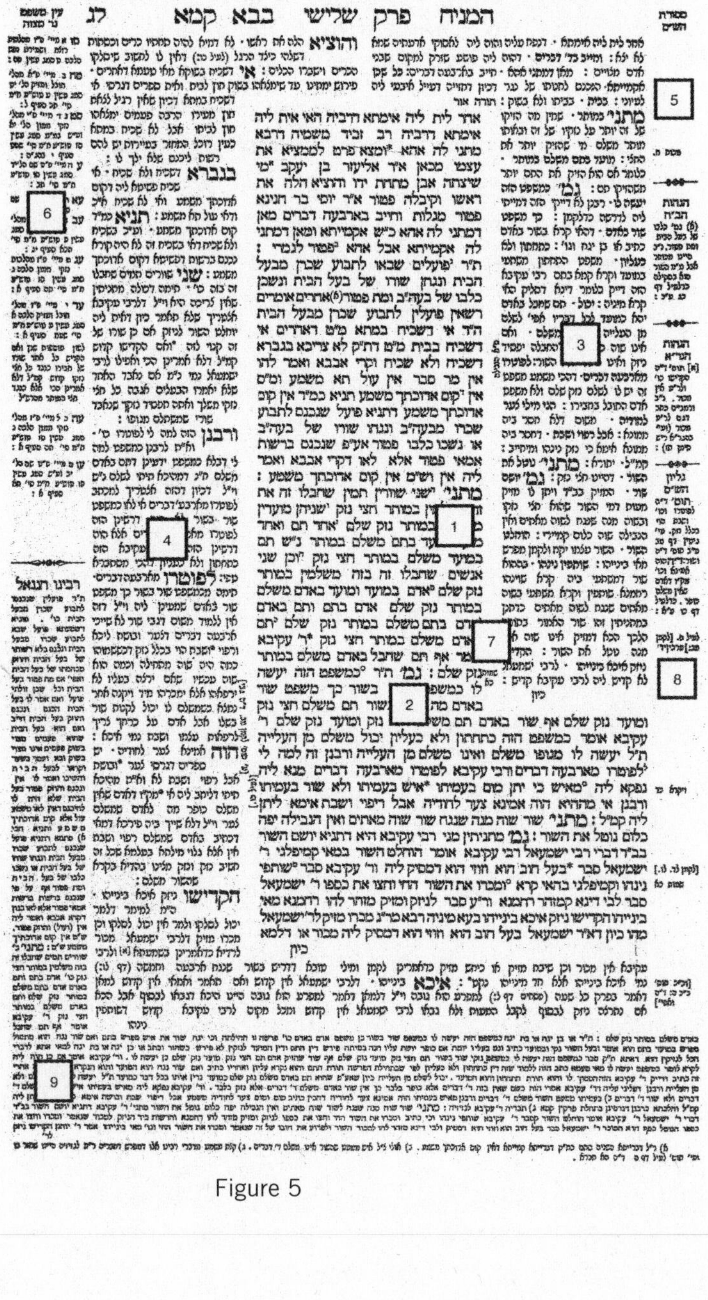

Figure 5

DISCUSSION QUESTIONS,

1. Discuss your level of comfort or discomfort with the degree to which people of faith comply with teachings in Genesis—Deuteronomy about treatment of the natural world.

2. Discuss whether you believe any closer adherence to those laws is possible by individual farmers and ranchers given corporate influence over forestry and agriculture.

3. Discuss whether clergy should call for greater adherence to the laws of which Jesus spoke. If not, why not?

4. How do you understand the difference between what you believe and what you know?

5. Consider beliefs you hold as certainties.

11

Beyond Deuteronomy:
Clearing the Air

A ir pollution has existed since biblical times, emanating, at that time, from sources such as tanneries and dead animals, and has become an increasingly disturbing part of our lives since the beginning of the Industrial Revolution. Up until the mid-1950s, we assumed the effects of pollutants were local effects—we could see it, feel it sting our eyes and burn our throats. We did not realize it was also sickening the atmosphere above us, and that illness, called the greenhouse effect, is fundamentally different from what we experienced in the past.

The fossil fuel emissions that have slowly been enlarging the earth's greenhouse canopy take centuries to diminish. That is why the term "irreversible" is used and explains why the goal for climate change mitigation is expressed as limiting the global average temperature to a degree or two Celsius above the long-term average.[1] Because the global average temperature is related to the amount of CO_2 in the atmosphere (ppm), and because the CO_2 remains in the atmosphere for centuries, that global average temperature will persist for centuries, or move higher.[2] Our children, grandchildren, and more distant descendants will be forced to adjust their agriculture, air travel,

---

1. James Hansen urges limiting the global average to a 1-degree temperature increase because of the likely irreparable damage to our planet should we reach a 2-degree temperature difference. See "Assessing 'Dangerous Climate Change': Required Reduction of Carbon Emissions to Protect Young People, Future Generations and Nature," James Hansen et. al., March 12, 2013, http://journals.plos.org/plosone/article?id=10.1371/journal.pone.0081648.

2. The global average temperature is already about 0.85 degrees above the average for the period 1880–2012: IPCC, 2013: Summary for Policymakers. In: *Climate Change 2013: The Physical Science Basis. Contribution of Working Group 1 to the Fifth Assessment Report of the Intergovernmental Panel on Climate Change* [Stocker, T.F., D. Qin, G.K. Plattner, M. Tignor, S.K. Allen, J. Boschung, A. Nauels, Y. Xia, V. Bex and P.M. Midgley (eds.)]. Cambridge University Press, Cambridge, United Kingdom and New York, NY, USA, 5.

habitable shoreline, energy infrastructure, and much more, to cope with the less hospitable, less familiar planet. The temperature will only slowly drop as we stop supplying the constituent gasses, such as CO_2.

Moreover, the effects of this greenhouse are not just local, but global. What we contribute to the greenhouse canopy affects the entire planet. Since the U.S. has one of the highest rates of emissions per capita, we bear a particular responsibility for corrective actions. And we can trace that responsibility back to biblical teachings.

The teaching of Jesus given in Matthew 7:12, "In everything do to others as you would have them do to you; for this is the law and the prophets" serves as a principle to guide our actions: it calls us to consider whether what we do to others we would welcome being done to us. The release of greenhouse gases into the atmosphere from our use of fossil fuels inflicts on others, and us, results such as droughts; forest fires; reduced food production; tornados, hurricanes, and storm surges; diseases from increased insect populations; fatalities from extreme heat—the list could go on.

This assertion of cause and effect is made with a high level of confidence, for the September 2013 report[3] from a group within the IPCC reinforces earlier conclusions by that panel on the human influences on climate change. Recent climate changes have had widespread impacts on human and natural systems. This perspective was forcefully reiterated in the opening pages of the IPCC Fifth Assessment Synthesis Report: "Human influence on the climate system is clear, and recent anthropogenic emissions of greenhouse gases are the highest in history." Thus, given what we now know, our use of fossil fuels for energy not only damages the air, land, water, and all life on earth, but also violates a principle derivable from biblical teachings. That principle rests, in part, on biblical verses such as Matthew 7:12 and others cited earlier, namely, ". . . you shall love your neighbor as yourself" (Lev. 19:18) and "You shall love your neighbor as yourself." (Matt. 22:39), (Mark 12:31).

If we question how far the concept of "neighbor" extends, we find this view from H.R. Niebuhr:

> Who, finally, is my neighbor, the companion whom I am commanded to love as myself or as I have been loved by my most loyal neighbor . . ?
>   . . . He is man and he is angel and he is animal and inorganic being, all that participates in being.[4]

---

3. IPCC, 2013: Summary for Policymakers, 11–15.

4. H. Richard Niebuhr, Daniel Day Williams, and James M. Gustafson, "The Purpose of the Church and its Ministry," *www.religion-online.org/showchapter.asp?title=407&C=151.*

The teachings from Leviticus, found also in Matthew, and Mark, influenced scholars who offered regulations about actions permitted within communities. Since air pollution existed in biblical times, we venture beyond Deuteronomy to the writers of the extensive commentary called the Talmud that includes the following regulation:[5]

> Carrion, graves, and tanyards [tanneries] must be kept fifty cubits[6] from a town. A tanyard must only be placed on the east side of a town.[7] [Because the east wind is gentle and will not carry the fumes into the town].

As with decaying bodies, the smell from the hide-tanning operation would be unpleasant, possibly unhealthful, and therefore must be distant from the town and downwind.

Elsewhere in the commentary one can find a number of rulings exemplifying the same principle:

- A stable could not be adjacent to a wine warehouse, because the odor from the stable would permeate the wine barrels.
- Paint storage could not be near bakeries—the smell would get into the flour.

Air pollution rulings did not just concern odors, but substances as well: A fixed threshing floor[8] must be kept fifty cubits from a town.[9] This was to prevent wind-borne chaff from jeopardizing the health of the people in the town.

These rulings about odors and substances constrain one from acting in ways that adversely affect the community.

The constraints encountered in Genesis–Deuteronomy mostly speak to individual actions, and the commentary often extends the principles to communities. That is, parts of the Talmud act like case law: They explain how to resolve particular questions that arise from interactions within the community in a manner consistent with the teachings in the first five books of the Bible Christians and Jews hold sacred.

---

5. Generally speaking, instructions in the Talmud carry the same authority for observant Jews as those in Genesis–Deuteronomy.

6. A cubit is about 18 inches, based on the length of a man's forearm.

7. *Babylonia Talmud*, Baba Bathra 25a, Soncino Edition, 6021.

8. A threshing floor is a place where grain was separated from the straw and husks by beating it or having cattle walk upon it. Then winnowing forks were used to throw the mixture into the air, allowing the wind to blow away the chaff, leaving the grain on the floor. (See *www.gotquestions.org/threshing-floor.html*)

9. *Babylonian Talmud*, Baba Bathra 24b, Soncino Edition, 6020.

We can take these rulings a step further by proposing a principle from the different examples regarding tanneries, paint storage, chaff, and a stable: Individuals are not to engage in actions that injure the community. This principle, supported by the biblical texts cited, would play a role similar to "concern for the distress of living creatures" that was formulated from the numerous verses about the treatment of animals.

The biblical rulings about odors and substances are not arcane judgments, nor is the principle extrapolated from them. Rather, these form part of the foundational teachings of English and early American law: In *Blackstone's Commentaries*, the main legal reference for our founding fathers, we find:

> . . . if a person keeps his hogs . . . so near the house of another, that the stench of them incommodes [inconveniences] him and makes the air unwholesome, this is an injurious nuisance, as it deprives him of the use and benefit of his house. A like injury is, if one's neighbor exercises any offensive trade; as a tanner's, a tallow chandler's, or the like; for though these are lawful and necessary trades, yet they should be exercised in remote places.[10]

These extraordinarily relevant rulings could apply to contemporary abuses to a community such as:

- Fumes from manufacturing or chemical plants that foul the air of nearby residents;
- Wastewater from manufacturing and chemical plants that contaminates the drinking water of residents;
- Mercury and particulates from cement plants that contaminate the air and water of surrounding communities;
- Intense odors from hog farms that degrade the lives of residents downwind; and
- Emissions of greenhouse gases that harm the entire earthly community.

These practices violate both biblical teachings and the foundational rulings of English and American law. We stand on very solid ground in

---

10. William Blackstone and George Tucker, *Blackstone's Commentaries* (Philadelphia: William Young Birch and Abraham Small, Robert Carr, printer, 1803), 360. Sir William Blackstone (1723–80) was an English jurist, judge, and Tory politician, most noted for writing the *Commentaries on the Laws of England*. *https://books.google.com/books?id=hgsOAQAAMAAJ&pg =PA239&dq=blackstone%27s+commentaries+hogs+stench&hl=en&sa=X&ei=6FFZVb-HNsquog SciYGYCQ&ved=0CB4Q6AEwAA#v=onepage&q=blackstone's%20commentaries%20hogs%20 stench&f=false*

calling for an end to such practices and, particularly, to emissions that harm *all* our neighbors.

People who hold the Bible sacred and those who support the rule of law can invoke these ancient, enduring principles in opposing the release of such a magnitude of greenhouse gases that they bring about the destruction, deaths, and injuries listed earlier.

Lynn White Jr.'s 1966 prediction about a worsening ecological crisis has come true, and I believe that part of the reason arises from observing that while humans do well at responding to immediate danger—"There's a saber-toothed tiger in the bushes!"—we do poorly at dealing with long-range consequences—"If you don't use good sunscreen, you'll get skin cancer by age fifty." Thus, from one perspective, remaining cognizant of biblical teachings compensates for our inherent limitations. That is, the teachings continually remind us both of how we are expected to behave in order to carry out our part of the covenant with the divine, and how to live in the world we were given.

The multiple verses about behavior with respect to the environment form part of what it means to live in relationship with the divine ("I make this covenant, with its sanctions, . . ."). It forms part of what distinguishes us. We perceive the capabilities of God as without limit—ours, however, have limits. As we recall from the first transgression and early teaching in Genesis 2: We lived in the Garden of Eden, in paradise, yet there was one thing we could not do, one limit to our autonomy:

> And the LORD God commanded the man, "You may freely eat of every tree of the garden; but of the tree of the knowledge of good and evil you shall not eat, for in the day that you eat of it you shall die."
>
> Gen. 2:16–17

Thus, even in the Garden of Eden, God placed a limitation on our interactions with the natural world.

Collectively, then, Genesis–Deuteronomy call us to:

- Preserve all species—preserve biological diversity;
- Manifest a concern for the distress of living creatures;
- Remain mindful of how the animals we eat were treated when alive;
- Do not destroy what still has use;
- Connect the practice of agriculture to caring for the needy;
- Maintain distinctions with both species and crops;

- Love your neighbor as yourself;
- Do not engage in an activity that injures the community;
- Pay attention.

The command to pay attention ("Hear O Israel," or "Listen you God-wrestlers") forms part of what Jesus identified as the most important teaching. If we pay attention to the changes on our planet and to forecasts of future changes and their effects, we witness the results of causative behavior strikingly at variance with biblical teachings.

We can synthesize the nine environmental instructions given above into a statement that stands in marked contrast to the wide latitude we interpret comes from Genesis 1:28:

> *Our latitude with respect to treatment of the natural world requires us to see each member (human, fish, animal, bird, tree, mustard seed) as created by God and to see each constraint relevant to our faith as a cord that potentially connects us personally to the divine and to the part of creation affected by the constraint.*

Adopting a perspective on the natural world reflecting this synthesis would change the relationship between humans and creation from one often mutually destructive to one truly symbiotic. For example, we destroy the earth's heat balance through emissions of greenhouse gases, and in turn experience lethal heat waves, crop-damaging droughts, fires, tornados, and more. If we start to restore that heat balance, the rains, crops, and indigenous species will begin returning to balance.

One perspective on our interpretation of Genesis 1:28, that we can do with the earth as we wish, does not even fully apply within the Garden Of Eden, for "the LORD God commanded the man, . . . but of the tree of the knowledge of good and evil you shall not eat." We saw a problem with the interpretation again in Genesis 7 ("And Noah did just as God commanded him," rather than Noah deciding which species to save and which to let perish in the flood) and verse after verse that clarify our behavior toward creation.

Another interpretation of Genesis 1:28 is that the word translated as "have dominion over" or "rule" means to be a good ruler, a good steward. Would God complete the work of creation and instruct us to rule over the newly created life forms in a way that damages what has just been created? It is implicit in the verse to be a good ruler, as Richard Elliott Friedman points out.[11] The multiple instructions that follow in Genesis–Deuteronomy, many of which have been cited, teach how we are to fulfill being a good ruler.

Thus, the prevailing interpretation of Genesis 1:28 is an incorrect summary of the environmental teachings in the Bible's first five books and, consequently, so are all practices based on it.

Biblical teachings about our interactions with the natural world occur, in part, to enable both humans and non-humans to maintain their particular covenant with God.

The environmental teachings touched upon connect with a broad range of critical problems, including climate change, endangered species, toxic waste, animal slaughtering practices, and air pollution. As Christians and Jews confront how to deal with each, may we include within our thinking the instructions about our actions with respect to the natural world that come from the core text that undergirds our religious beliefs.

As we confront each problem and assess its urgency, we do well to recall these teachings from the Gospel of Matthew:

> "Truly I tell you, just as you did it to one of the least of these who are members of my family, you did it to me."

Matt.:25:40b

> "Truly I tell you, just as you did not do it to one of the least of these, you did not do it to me."

Matt.:25:45b

Climate change will afflict the needy earliest and hardest, for they have the least ability to adapt. The middle class and the wealthy can better cover high air conditioning costs, can add insulation and improve windows in their residences in order to block the heat, and can more easily move inland from coastal communities at risk from storm surges. With respect to climate change, delaying a speedy transition from fossil fuels to renewables and nuclear energy will inflict pain first and hardest on "the least of these," and we are accountable for our actions.

We have the capacity to lessen the effects of climate change. The situation is not hopeless, though the problem presents an unprecedented level of urgency. Our task is to respond to both the scientific data at hand and the tenets of our faith with a passion and energy that befits the problem.

---

11. Richard Elliott Friedman, *Commentary on the Torah* (San Fransico: HarperSanFrancisco, 2001), 13.

DISCUSSION QUESTIONS

1. As people of faith, what are we called to do to maintain our part of the covenantal relationship with God?

2. Discuss the connection, as you interpret it, between air pollution in biblical times and air pollution today, including emissions of carbon dioxide.

3. Discuss the synthesis offered in this chapter in light of the teaching given by the hymn, "This Is My Father's World."[12]

4. Discuss the differences between the prevailing interpretation of Genesis 1:28 and the synthesis of this chapter.

12. *The Hymnal* (New York: Church Publishing, 1982). #651.

Part II

A Call to Action—National Level

12

Rate of Change

The opening words of the commandment Jesus cited as the most important (Matt. 22:37) derive from Deuteronomy 6:4 and are the same words Jews affirm in every service: *Hear O Israel*.[1] Colloquially, *listen Israel, pay attention*! Pay attention! Consider: If the Divine wants to communicate with us, the first step is to secure our attention.

Attention should be unavoidable when:

- The globally averaged temperature over land and ocean surfaces in 2014 was the highest since record keeping began in 1880, and was the thirty-eighth consecutive year in which global temperatures were higher than the twentieth-century average. The ten warmest years ever recorded all occurred since 1998[2];

- Texas sweltered under the warmest weather any U.S. state ever experienced during June–August 2011, and in September–October unprecedented fires torched the state: "No one on the face of this Earth has ever fought fires in these extreme conditions."[3] Intense fires occur more frequently because climate change includes effects such as high temperatures that stress trees, inadequate rainfall, and attacks by pests that multiply faster in a warmer environment;

- California experienced unprecedented conditions of drought in 2012–2014, and in May 2014 a fire of historic proportions ravaged over 10,000 acres in the area of San Diego County. Three dozen fires raged one evening and eight continued into the following day, when temperatures hovered around 100 degrees;

1. Hear, O Israel: the Lord is our God, the Lord alone.
2. http://climate.nasa.gov/blog/2224 .
3. In a press release from the Texas Forest Service, September 6, 2011; reported by CBS News.

- During April–May 2011, flooding along the Mississippi River was the largest and most damaging along any U.S. waterway in the past century;
- The European heat wave of June–August 2003 was the hottest experienced since records began in 1780 and, according to one researcher, "is very likely to have been the hottest summer since at least 1500."[4] The heat wave was responsible for more than 70,000 deaths, with France particularly hard hit, experiencing over 14,000 heat-related fatalities;
- A historic number of tornadoes in 2011 took a devastating toll on numerous U.S. states. These included: the April 14–16 period with 178 confirmed tornadoes affecting 16 states, and killing 38 people; the April 25–28 outbreak that killed 349 people across 6 states; April 27, the most destructive tornado day in U.S. history with a record 205 events; and the monster tornado of May 22 that struck Joplin, Missouri, killing 116 people, destroying about 7,000 homes, delivering peak winds of 225–250 mph, and stretching more than one mile across at its maximum.

And this list does not include less dramatic, but equally difficult, changes such as higher summer temperatures and more frequent problems occasioned by sea-level rise, for which the ground-zero location in the U.S. is, apparently, the state of Florida. The earth is, quite literally, claiming our attention. This explains why the number of people who believe in climate change is on the rise, according to a recent survey.[5] We don't need to debate the science, we're feeling the effects.

Sea water is entering the Biscayne Aquifer, which provides water for most of densely populated South Florida.[6] Salt water has already crept six miles inland in Broward County and is likely to continue this incursion.[7]

---

4. K.E. Trenberth, P.D. Jones, P. Ambenje, R. Bojariu, D. Easterling, A. Klein Tank, D. Parker, F. Rahimzadeh, J.A. Renwick, M. Rusticucci, B. Soden and P. Zhai, 2007: Observations: Surface and Atmospheric Climate Change. In: *Climate Change 2007: The Physical Science Basis, 311.* Contribution of Working Group I to the Fourth Assessment Report of the Intergovernmental Panel on Climate Change [Solomon, S., D. Qin, M. Manning, Z. Chen, M. Marquis, K.B. Averyt, M. Tignor and H.L. Miller (eds.)]. Cambridge University Press, Cambridge, United Kingdom and New York, NY, USA.

5. *The Week* (May 11, 2012), 21.

6. *Climate Change and Sea-Level Rise in Florida* (Tallahassee: The Florida Oceans and Coastal Council, December 2010).

7. *http://www.dailykos.com/story/2015/03/19/1372031/-The-phenomenon-that-can-not-be-spoken-in-Florida-continues-as-salt-water-intrusion-moves-inland#*

Irrefutable evidence of the threat from sea level rise also exists in, for example, Miami Beach, where spring and autumn high tides now bring walls of seawater that inundate the area's west side and flow into the city's storm drains.[8] Another foot of sea level rise, predicts the mayor of South Miami, could launch a sequence of cascading events that include: the inability to flush away sewage; water taps unable to deliver fresh water to homes; the unavailability of flood insurance; a precipitous drop in property values and a loss of population; and insufficient tax revenues to fund police, fire, and other essential city services.

This almost apocalyptic scenario does not seem to phase the deniers of climate change in the state's Republican leadership, such as the governor (in 2014), a former governor, and one of the state's senators. The city is investing about $1.5 billion to improve the troubled drain and sewer systems, which is good, but the denial from state political leadership makes it difficult to address the problem in the comprehensive fashion required.

Extreme weather events are one predictable outcome of climate change, according to the Intergovernmental Panel on Climate Change (IPCC). And as America's pre-eminent climate scientist, James Hansen, put it, it is inappropriate "to repeat the caveat that no individual weather event can be directly linked to climate change . . . there is virtually no explanation other than climate change."[9] It is likely that we will endure an increasing number of these as the earth continues to warm.[10]

To gain additional perspective on extreme weather events, a look back fifty years reveals that we experienced an average of 608 tornados for the decade of the 1960s, with a minimum number of 493 in 1963 and a maximum of 995 in 1965. In contrast, 2011 saw more than 1,562 events, and the year 2012 blew past that with 1,625 tornados, both more than double the average for the 1960s.[11]

Why is this happening? The root cause is the increase in emissions of carbon dioxide (CO_2) into the atmosphere.

---

8. The information that follows came from a comprehensive article in The Guardian: *http://www.theguardian.com/world/2014/jul/11/miami-drowning-climate-change-deniers-sea-levels-rising*

9. James E. Hansen, "Climate Change Is Here—And Worse Than We Thought," *Washington Post,* August 3, 2012, *http://www.washingtonpost.com/opinions/climate-change-is-here--and-worse-than-we-thought/2012/08/03/6ae604c2-dd90-11e1-8e43-4a3c4375504a_story.html.*

10. The IPCC Fourth Assessment Report, page 310, expresses this cautiously: "It may be possible, however, to say that the occurrence of recent events is consistent with physically based expectations arising from climate change."

11. *http://www4.ncdc.noaa.gov/cgi-win/wwcgi.dll?wwevent-storms.*

Our knowledge about the presence of CO_2 in the upper atmosphere has increased over the past half-century due to measurements taken by numerous researchers. In particular, the data of C.D. Keeling of the Scripps Institute of Oceanography and John Chin of the Mauna Loa Observatory in Hawaii, possibly the most comprehensive and accurate, reveal a steady buildup in CO_2 from about 315 ppm[12] in 1959 to 400 ppm in 2013.

In the pre-industrial period, perhaps up to the year 1750, measurements and calculations place CO_2 at 275–285 ppm. CO_2 increased by 50 ppm by the 1970s, a period of about 200 years. The second 50 ppm increase occurred in just 30 years. Then, in the 10 years from 2000–2010, atmospheric CO_2 increased by about 20 ppm, the highest average growth rate recorded for any decade since direct measurements began in the 1950s.

Consider the *rate of change* these figures reveal. Up to the 1970s, the increase in CO_2 was about 0.25 ppm per year (50 ppm over 200 years). Over the next 30 years, the increase averaged 1.66 ppm per year. In the last decade, the increase averaged 2 ppm per year, or a rate almost 10 times faster than in the 200-year period first mentioned. This change in the *rate of change* (0.25 to 2) cannot be attributed to naturally occurring climate variation, but results from external factors easily identified: increasing amounts of CO_2 have been sent into the atmosphere through the combustion of coal at electricity generating stations, through the combustion of fuel in our cars and airplanes, and in multiple other ways.

Recall that the CO_2, whose rate of change has increased ten-fold in 200 years, acts like the glass in a greenhouse, reflecting back to earth some of the radiated heat that would otherwise vent into space. Increasing amounts of CO_2, as well as methane, nitrous oxide, and other gases, reflect back to earth increasing amounts of heat radiated toward space. This results in a warming of the planet which, in turn, brings about a change in the climate. The U.S. ranks as one of the largest emitters, both in total emissions and per capita: 5490 million metric tons (MMT) (2011) and 17.28 metric tons (MT) per capita (2009). China contributes 8715 MMT (2011) and 5.77 MT per capita (2009).[13]

---

12. The number of CO_2 molecules in one million molecules of dry air. *http://www.esrl.noaa.gov/gmd/ccgg/about/co2_measurements.html.*

13. *www.indexmundi.com/facts/indicators/EN.ATM.CO2E.PC/rankings. www.eia.gov/cfapps/ipdb project/iedindex3.cfm?tid=90&pid=44&aid=8.*

Perhaps an analogy will further clarify this notion of rate of change. Consider a boy on his tenth birthday who—within a month—changes—physically, emotionally, and mentally into a boy of eleven years of age. That is, by all physical and mental measures this person now appears to have aged by one year in the span of one month. Let's further consider that one month later this boy now appears to be twelve years of age, by all the same measures. And again, four weeks later this boy now appears to be thirteen years old. We would know that something is terribly wrong. It's true, of course, that children do reach the ages of eleven, twelve, and thirteen, but within intervals of one, two, and three years, not one, two, and three months. That's analogous to the disturbing rate of change we are observing with multiple features of our planet.

Figure 6 (overleaf) from the Technical Summary of the Fourth Assessment IPCC report of 2007 provides compelling evidence of the correlation of human activities with the temperature difference (labeled "Temperature anomaly") between that observed and the long-term average.[14]

Focusing attention on the three plots at the bottom of Figure 6 reveals two shaded areas in each, with the shaded areas identified below the plots. These areas overlap up to about 1950, but then diverge as the accumulated effects of human activities began to manifest themselves on the climate.

Each shaded area illustrates the range of results from simulations with several climate models; that is, each climate model's simulation does not yield precisely the same temperature anomaly, but the variation of results is included in a narrow band that is represented by the shaded area.

The black line in each of the three plots represents the observed tempetature difference from 1906 to 2000. This black line lies within the shaded area labeled "Models using both natural and anthropogenic forcings." Anthropogenic (or human-induced) forcings include the effects of emissions from coal-fired power plants, gasoline-powered cars, and other sources.

---

14. Solomon, S., D. Qin, M. Manning, R.B. Alley, T. Berntsen, N.L. Bindoff, Z. Chen, A. Chidthaisong, J.M. Gregory, G.C. Hegerl, M. Heimann, B. Hewitson, B.J. Hoskins, F. Joos, J. Jouzel, V. Kattsov, U. Lohmann, T. Matsuno, M. Molina, N. Nicholls, J. Overpeck, G. Raga, V. Ramaswamy, J. Ren, M. Rusticucci, R. Somerville, T.F. Stocker, P. Whetton, R.A. Wood and D. Wratt, 2007: Technical Summary, 61. In: *Climate Change 2007: The Physical Science Basis. Contribution of Working Group I to the Fourth Assessment Report of the Intergovernmental Panel on Climate Change* [Solomon, S., D. Qin, M. Manning, Z. Chen, M. Marquis, K.B. Averyt, M. Tignor and H.L. Miller (eds.)]. Cambridge University Press, Cambridge, United Kingdom and New York, NY, USA. Used with permission.

GLOBAL AND CONTINENTAL TEMPERATURE CHANGE

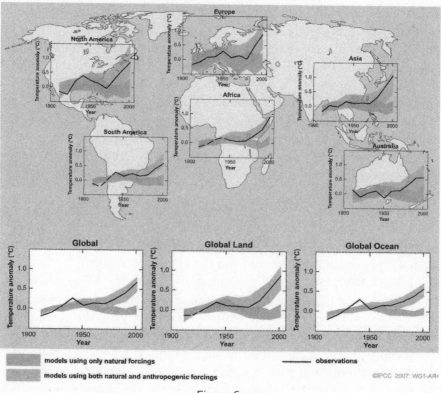

Figure 6

This model correlates so well with actual temperature over the entire century that the IPCC calls the warming of the climate system due to human activity "very likely"[15] and the warming of the climate system "unequivocal."

The human and animal populations of the earth have adapted over the centuries to their geographic locations, one primary characteristic of which is the climate: the seasonal temperatures, winds, rainfall, and storms. While the annual characteristics of the climate do change, they have historically done so over time periods orders of magnitude greater than the life spans of the human and animal populations. This has enabled the species on earth to adapt to such slow-moving shifts. Changes in climate that occur in decades rather than millennia can cause enormous pain to all life on earth.

---

15. IPCC, Technical Summary, Fourth Assessment Report, 60.

What can we do to alleviate this pain? First, who's the *we*? Who are the people who want to prevent these devastating consequences of climate change and the deaths, injuries, destruction, and financial losses that accompany them? This book has been addressing Christians and Jews who are people of faith, people whose lives are shaped, to varying degrees, by biblical teachings. Some in this group believe climate change is causing the effects observed, while others remain unconvinced. People of faith agree, however, that many of the causative actions described in Part I are at odds with biblical instructions, and they share a desire to end such transgressions.

That's one part of the core constituency, the *we*. The second group includes those people who accept the evidence of climate change and the predictions of devastating future consequences, but for whom religious faith is not a compelling force.

These two parts comprise a huge group, more than enough people to bring about change in a democratic society. However, with significant amounts of money and short-term thinking playing such strong roles among those who would deny these realities and minimize their consequences, change will not come easily. That's rather obvious. Just as important is the crucial distinction between individuals and collectives; that is, between individuals and the federal government, state governments, or for-profit corporations. It is these institutions that must enact or undergo the changes that will result in fewer greenhouse gas (GHG) emissions venting into the atmosphere. The power of governments and corporations far exceed the power of individuals. However, Americans know how to deal with this disparity in power, and we have evidence of effective strategies to overcome it and prevail. We'll return to this point shortly.

The changes called for include reducing greenhouse gas emissions from coal-fired electricity generating stations and from the use of conventional motor fuels, with the real goal of ending the use of fossil fuels as energy sources before the year 2050.[16] The second goal is to capture carbon through reforestation. Carbon capture becomes more difficult each year, as fires facilitated by high temperatures and drought destroy tens of thousands of acres of forest, sending their carbon skywards and ending their capacity to function as carbon sinks. The Texas fires of 2011 and the Colorado fires of 2012 serve as two examples.

Bill McKibben makes a compelling case in an article in *Rolling Stone* that our atmosphere cannot take more than 565 gigatons of carbon before

---

16. See "The Reckoning," by Bill McKibben, *Rolling Stone*, July 19, 2012, 52, 54–58, 60.

our planet becomes unbearably hot and violent, with inadequate food for the inhabitants. The business plan of energy companies, not by intent but by default, targets just such a planet. They must rapidly phase out selling fossil fuels and use their vast wealth to develop alternative sources.

Targeting the destruction of our life-support system in business plans expands the climate change crisis into a religious/spiritual issue, as well as a secular one, and thereby connects with the thesis of Part I: We cannot simultaneously be people of faith and engage in actions that result in the ravaging of creation.

McKibben identifies two key strategies: putting a tax on fossil fuels, and encouraging pension funds, universities, churches, and similar entities to divest their holdings in energy companies.

A price on carbon is precisely what was *requested* by six European oil companies in a letter to the co-chairs of the 2015 U.N. conference on climate change. This is discussed further in chapter 14.

The divestment campaign has been remarkably successful, with over $50 billion invested in fossil fuel companies dropped from the portfolios of 180 organizations.[17] A particularly notable action occurred in February 2015 when Norway's Government Pension Fund Global (GPFG), the world's wealthiest at $850 billion, divested from 22 companies because of their involvement with high carbon emissions and from 16 coal companies linked to deforestation in Indonesia and India.

"Our risk-based approach means that we exit sectors and areas where we see elevated levels of risk to our investments in the long term," said a spokesperson for GPFG, as quoted in *The Guardian*. "Companies with particularly high greenhouse gas emissions may be exposed to risk from regulatory or other changes leading to a fall in demand."

Placing such financial pressure on energy companies is reminiscent of the strategy of divestment that played a key role in ending apartheid in South Africa. This financial pressure may reduce the army of lobbyists that has been successful at destroying political initiatives to attack climate change, may enable our government and others around the world to take the steps necessary to protect the world population, and may persuade energy companies to invest in renewable and nuclear energy and thereby attract former and new investors.

---

17. *http://www.theguardian.com/environment/2015/feb/05/worlds-biggest-sovereign-wealth-fund-dumps-dozens-of-coal-companies*

13

Societal Transformation

Reducing energy demands and changing energy sources involves a societal transformation, in particular how much coal, oil, and natural gas we use, compared to solar, wind, and nuclear, and the infrastructure reconfiguration necessary to accommodate these more environmentally friendly sources. In particular, we need to transform how we generate electricity. About 39 percent of our electricity comes from 300 coal-fired power plants.[1] That number of plants needs to drop sharply and quickly, and not solely by converting them to natural gas plants.

Our society needs to develop alternatives to conventional motor fuels (electric and hybrid cars still tap into the grid in one form or another) and to engage in massive reforestation projects; a 2011 paper by James Hansen, America's pre-eminent climatologist, and several others[2] reports that one of the measures that would help slow climate change is to capture carbon through major reforestation, with the goal of capturing 100 gigatons of CO_2 over fifty years.

In addition, the ability to be recycled must be built into non-consumable products in order to reduce the energy and materials needed to generate new ones. How can we accomplish this within the next few decades before we pass a point of no return, that is, a point where our planet will inevitably become unbearably hot and violent?

---

1. Energy Information Administration: 39 percent is the 2014 figure. *www.eia.gov/tools/faqs/faq.cfm?id=427&t=3*. 300 coal-fired electricity plants is the 2013 figure. *www.eia.gov/electricity/annual/html/epa_04_01.html*.

2. "The Case for Young People and Nature: A Path to a Healthy, Natural, Prosperous Future"; James Hansen, Pushker Kharecha, Makiko Sato, Paul Epstein, Paul J. Hearty, Ove Hoegh-Guldberg, Camille Parmesan, Stefan Rahmstorf, Johan Rockstrom, Eelco J. Rohling, Jeffrey Sachs, Peter Smith, Konrad Steffen, Karina von Schuckmann, James C. Zachos. *http://www.columbia.edu/~jeh1/mailings/2011/20110505_CaseForYoungPeople.pdf*.

A look back in America's recent past reveals a similar drive toward transformation, the move to racial equality. The goals of the civil rights movement of the mid-twentieth century included equality in job opportunities, housing choices, education, voting rights, and access to public and private facilities. It was—and remains—a massive undertaking, but one in which our *legislative* course to racial equality was substantially locked in within two decades, from about 1955 to 1975.

[A necessary aside: The several killings of African-American men by law enforcement agents under highly questionable circumstances in 2014 and 2015 signal that our society has not achieved the racial equality that our legislative structure enables. Moreover, the voting rights aspect of that structure has been weakened by a decision of the Supreme Court and regressive actions by several state legislatures. The fact that our first African American president was elected twice by clear majorities of both the popular vote and the Electoral College suggests that our country as a whole has achieved an admirable level of racial impartiality. But the residual racial prejudice has likely been inflamed during President Obama's tenure. We need to find ways to accelerate racial harmony throughout our society.]

The strategist and driving force behind the transformation from segregation to integration was the Rev. Dr. Martin Luther King Jr., a Baptist minister. It's notable that the movement was led by Dr. King and fellow Baptist clergy and subsequently supported by other clergy, for none of the above objectives was a religious one, at least not on the surface. But just below the surface, absolutely, these were religious issues.

A core issue was the equality and dignity of each individual. Defending racial segregation and the limitations and indignities it imposed was to assert a difference in the worth of one individual over another. Nothing in the Bible supports this, and clergy of all denominations were on solid ground in asserting their support of integration. Of course, it took some clergy a long time to recall this teaching.

We cannot afford for clergy to take much longer to understand the religious aspects of climate change and to confront the issue with their congregations, for greenhouse gases increase each day and with them the threat to preserving a hospitable planet. As the Rev. Fletcher Harper expressed it, "If religion cannot provide meaningful leadership on one of the most pressing issues facing the human family, then it will lose its ability to present itself as a moral force."[3] Thus, organized religion is being tested. Either it exercises leadership because of the religious and physical imperatives of climate change or it reveals its inability to serve as a "moral force." The teachings will remain sacred, but the institutions will be revealed as demonstrably incompetent in regard to the sacred obligation of creation care.

Genesis–Deuteronomy contains thirty-six variations of "You shall treat the stranger as the native," a teaching repeated more than any other. This was spoken from pulpits in synagogues and churches throughout the civil rights movement. The descendants of the Africans forcibly brought to this country more than a century ago were assuredly now among the home-born. Different treatment, whether viewed as home-born or stranger, violated a central biblical teaching.

The memory that Jews hold of their release from Egyptian bondage, a story repeated each Passover, fostered close cooperation between Jews and African Americans during the civil rights movement. Joachim Prinz, president of the American Jewish Congress at the time, forcefully articulated this bond when he spoke from the Lincoln Memorial during the famous March on Washington on August 28, 1963:

> As Jews we bring to this great demonstration, in which thousands of us proudly participate, a two-fold experience—one of the spirit and one of History. . . . From our Jewish historic experience of three and a half thousand years we say: Our ancient history began with slavery and the yearning for freedom. During the Middle Ages my people lived for a thousand years in the ghettos of Europe. . . . It is for these reasons that it is not merely sympathy and compassion for the black people of America that motivates us. It is above all and beyond all such sympathies and emotions a sense of complete identification and solidarity born of our own painful historic experience.[4]

The combination of the core issue of the equal worth of each individual and the shared text of the book of Exodus drew Christian clergy from multiple denominations to deliver a similar message that segregation violated the tenets of our faith. An increasing number of us pressed for federal and

---

3. "I Believe Three Things," in *Love God Heal Earth*, The Rev. Canon Sally G. Bingham, St. Lynn's Press, Pittsburgh, PA, 2009, 165.

4. *www.joachimprinz.com/civilrights.htm* Used with permission.

state changes that would deliver equality in education, housing, and jobs. The religious message added fuel to the movement for change.

A similar situation exists with climate change. Substitute reducing greenhouse gas emissions for legislative efforts toward ending racial segregation. Segregation penetrated multiple parts of our basic societal structure, such as housing, education, public transportation, and employment. That is why it required a transformation of our society to end the numerous manifestations of that corrosive policy. A list of climate objectives characterizing the changes needed easily mirror the five equality objectives for integration. In addition, for Christians and Jews, at least, climate change is clearly also a religious issue. These similarities lead to the next logical step responsive to the crisis at hand.

14

A Call to Action

The Environmental Protection Agency (EPA) and the Food and Drug Administration (FDA) are charged with, among other responsibilities, protecting the quality of the air we breathe, the water we drink, and the food we eat. Over the decades, I believe the agencies have tried mightily to fulfill their mission. The record compiled, however, reveals that for reasons familiar to many, the agencies have not always succeeded. The reasons include:

- Budget cuts, often in response to corporate pressures, crippling enforcement;
- The revolving door: the regulated becoming the regulator, and corrupting the process; and,
- The alteration of scientific conclusions, undermining the justification for action.

Thus, we have adjusted to air that is polluted by smog originating from automobile exhaust; emissions from oil refineries, chemical plants, or concrete plants; and smoke from coal-fired power plants. We have adjusted to water that smells of chlorine because of the treatment required to neutralize the effects of bacteria/chemicals from agricultural runoff, oil from roadways, leftover drugs poured into the sewer system, and multiple other sources. We have adjusted to food containing, particularly for children, questionably acceptable residues of pesticides and insecticides; meat and milk with residues of growth hormones and antibiotics: we can't even learn, in many cases, if the food we're eating contains genetically modified ingredients, such is the power of agribusiness.

Thus, like the proverbial frog in heated water, we've adjusted to polluted air, smelly water, genetically modified or compromised food. For decades, we have adjusted.

But the climate crisis ratchets up the stakes. Now we are being asked to adjust to virtual extinction. Yes, the great ball of earth will continue to orbit the sun, but it won't be teeming with life, and for the humans on board the "quality of life" will be a shadow of what we know today.

Climate change calls for an environmental rights movement, a movement that asserts *we have the right to an environment that supports life*. We won't adjust to extinction.

This assertion harmonizes with the mission of Our Children's Trust, which seeks "to secure the legal right to a healthy atmosphere and stable climate for all present and future generations."[1] The organization helps youth plaintiffs undertake legal action in the U.S. and abroad to require governments "to adopt and implement enforceable science-based Climate Recovery Plans."

When snow and ice disappear from mountain tops, we lose the seasonal run-off that irrigates our crops and quenches our thirst. When droughts strike, crop production drops for an ever-larger population and prices increase, hurting the poor. When forests burn, we lose the carbon-capture and oxygen-producing capacities of its trees and habitats for countless insects, land animals, and birds. When large amounts of water in lakes and rivers evaporate under intense heat, we lose water for irrigation and drinking. When the acidity of lakes and rivers increases, we reduce fish populations and, as a side effect, our food supply. This list could go on, leading one to see a future with global food production and potable water supplies reduced, bringing a drop in human and animal populations, and an aging electricity infrastructure increasingly unable to condition our buildings to comfortable temperatures, contributing, in turn, to heat-related deaths.

The environmental rights movement must be a movement larger, more sustained, and more forceful than anything yet undertaken, for the stakes are higher than anything we have faced before. If Bill McKibben's 2012 summary of climate findings is correct, and the huge body of scientific evidence it draws upon plus the painful facts on the ground suggest it is, we have less than one generation to accomplish changes that hold total atmospheric CO_2 to a manageable level.

While an environmental rights movement would function similarly to the civil rights movement, important differences would exist between the two. While the civil rights movement affected us personally (for example,

---

1. *http://ourchildrenstrust.org/Mission*. Used with permission.

who we sat with in a restaurant, movie theater, or bus, and who our children went to school with), an environmental rights movement will affect us primarily indirectly; most of us don't care whether our electricity comes from a coal-fired power plant or from a wind farm as long as the lights go on when we flip the switch. We don't care whether gasoline, natural gas, or fuel cells power our cars, as long as they take us where we wish to go and can be re-fueled when needed. However, from an environmental perspective we do care about the source of our electricity, for using a wind farm or nuclear energy rather than a coal plant means that five million metric tons less CO_2 (on average) would enter the atmosphere.

Of course, coal mining companies and the miners who work for them are impacted directly and do care about these changes. But opposing carbon reductions to keep miners employed and companies profitable is not the solution. That leads to devastation of the planet and economic hardships for America and other countries. We know how to reduce fossil fuel use and transition to other energy sources. We do not yet know how to navigate the employment and economic changes that will occur. It is past time for industry and government officials to face reality and address the truly tough issues.

Fortunately for the coal mining states, the Obama administration is facing that reality, as manifested by multiple actions, by including a $10 billion request to Congress in its FY 2016 budget to assist communities negatively impacted by changes in the coal industry and power sector. The administration asked Congress to fund The Partnerships for Opportunity and Workforce and Economic Revitalization (POWER) Initiative. In October 2015, the administration announced 36 awards totaling over $14 million for partnerships in 12 states and tribal nations, using existing funds.[2]

Equally important for the coal industry is to accelerate research into promising new markets for coal that do not involve burning it. One area, involving carbon fiber, is discussed in chapter 16.

The Rev. King's strategy for the civil rights movement was strongly influenced by pastor and educator Reinhold Niebuhr,[3] especially his book

---

2. The October announcement is described at: *https://www.whitehouse.gov/the-press-office/2015/10/15/fact-sheet-administration-announces-new-workforce-and-economic.*

3. Reinhold Niebuhr (1892–1971) was one of the most influential Christian theologians of the twentieth century. He was a professor of Christian ethics at the Union Theological Seminary for over thirty years, and dean from 1950–1960. Niebuhr was a powerful speaker, and often criticized religious liberals for what he viewed as their naïve perspective on human nature. His theological stance came to be described as Christian Realism.

Moral Man and Immoral Society, and Mohandas Gandhi[4] and his principle of nonviolence.

Niebuhr pointed out that we must recognize the difference between appeals to individuals and appeals to institutions, the point raised earlier. The Rev. King understood Niebuhr's teaching that people who advocate for moving from segregation to integration, based on both secular issues and religious teachings, must "recognize that when collective power, whether in the form of imperialism or class domination, exploits weakness, it can never be dislodged unless power is raised against it." The collective power during segregation was class domination, the white majority dominating the African-American minority.

The eloquence and clarity of the prose from Niebuhr's 1932 book merits quoting to understand why the second part of King's strategy was similar to the confrontational non-violence employed by Gandhi to lead India to freedom from British rule.

> Since reason is always, to some degree, the servant of interest in a social situation, social injustice cannot be resolved by moral and rational suasion alone, as the educator and social scientist usually believe. Conflict is inevitable, and in this conflict power must be challenged by power.[5]

> What is lacking among all these moralists, whether religious or rational, is an understanding of the brutal character of the behavior of all human collectives, and the power of self-interest and collective egoism in all intergroup relations. . . . They do not see that the limitations of the human imagination, the easy subservience of reason to prejudice and passion, and the consequent persistence of irrational egoism, particularly in group behavior, make social conflict an inevitability in human history, probably to its very end.[6]

This from a theologian!

The validity of this assertion by Niebuhr, and its alternate phrasing in the Introduction, is supported by three memorable examples:

---

4. Mohandas Gandhi (1869–1948) led India to independence from Great Britain in 1947, largely using tactics of confrontational non-violence. He was attracted to non-violence by both the Bhagavad Gita (Hindu sacred scripture) and the teachings of Jesus.

5. Reinhold Niebuhr, *Moral Man and Immoral Society: A Study in Ethics and Politics*, Charles Scribner's Sons, New York, 1932, xiv–xv.

6. Ibid., xx.

- published experimental evidence of the health risks from leaded gasoline (mental retardation in children, for example) did not dissuade some corporations from over twenty years of disputing the findings, and lobbying political leaders to take no action to address the problem. Professor Herbert Needleman, an academic involved for years with this issue, described a dinner meeting with an EPA representative and an executive from the company that made the gasoline additive. The gathering took place after the government had ordered a phase-out of the leaded gasoline additive. Needleman asked the executive why the company did not develop a safer additive. The response was that company economists estimated that leaded gasoline sales would soon level off or possibly decline, and, with that projection, an investment of perhaps $100 million was unwarranted. Needleman realized that the whole protracted debate about the accuracy of scientific studies was merely a "shadow play," a diversion. The company made an economic decision and their plan was simply not to budge on the additive for as long as possible, and challenge medical and environmental findings to support their position;[7]
- published experimental evidence of the widening hole in the ozone layer (see the footnote in chapter 8 about the Montreal Protocol) did not dissuade some corporations from more than ten years of disputing the findings and lobbying political leaders to take no action to deal with the problem;
- published medical findings of the connection between smoking and lung cancer did not dissuade some corporations from decades of disputing the findings and lobbying political leaders to take no action to deal with the problem.

The debate about the validity of climate change represents a fourth instance of "shadow play." Despite abundant physical evidence and published analyses by a large, diverse, international group of scientists, some corporate representatives and corporately funded think tanks continue to dispute the findings—*with no counter analysis*—and work to misinform the public about the severity of the problem and the substantive changes needed.[8]

---

7. Herbert L. Needleman, "The Removal of Lead from Gasoline: Historical and Personal Reflections," Environmental Research Section A 84, 20–35 (2000).

8. See, for example: *http://www.theguardian.com/environment/2012/may/08/conservative-thinktanks-obama-energy-plans*

Our capitalist society has apparently degenerated to the point where some corporations are willing to sacrifice the future habitability of the planet for short-term profit. This seems to me a profound perversion of the rules under which corporations may act.[9] We need to develop iron-clad rules that make such actions both unacceptable and illegal. And we must express outrage and lament our acceptance of this "shadow play" that jeopardizes our hospitable planet.

An article in the magazine *Onearth* titled "The Profits of Doom" includes the assertion that markets are amoral, not immoral, and that if governments develop appropriate frameworks, private capital can produce "enlightened" outcomes.[10] This would inspire hope were it not for the too-frequent actions of U.S. private capital, enabled by lobbying and money, to derail government efforts to craft "the right framework." Such behavior plunges from amoral to immoral when climate change and the future habitability of the planet are at stake. Sadly, corporate influence has been strengthened by highly regrettable Supreme Court decisions in Citizens United and McCutcheon.[11]

A surprising and major difference between our version of a capitalist society and European societies was revealed in June 2015, when six European oil company executives, but no American ones, acknowledged that continued increases in atmospheric CO_2 are incompatible with preserving a hospitable environment. The European companies *asked* the co-chairs planning the December 2015 U.N. meeting on climate change to impose a price on carbon as part of providing them with a clear and stable policy framework.[12] This European action supports the point

9. In a move sadly reminiscent of the prolonged inquiry into tobacco company statements about the effects of smoking on health, the New York State attorney general has launched an investigation of Exxon Mobil to determine whether information the company released about the effects of fossil fuels on climate change misled both investors and the public. See: Justin Gillis and Clifford Krauss, "Exxon Mobil Investigated for Possible Climate Change Lies by New York Attorney General," *New York Times,* November 5, 2015. *www.nytimes.com/2015/11/06/science/exxon-mobil-under-investigation-in-new-york-over-climate-statements.html?_r=0.*

10. George Black, "The Profits of Doom," *Onearth*, The Natural Resources Defense Council, Spring 2014, 58.

11. Citizens United v. Federal Election Commission, Supreme Court of the United States, decided January 21, 2010. McCutcheon et al v. Federal Election Commission, Supreme Court of the United States, decided April 2, 2014.

12. *http://www.reuters.com/article/2015/06/01/europe-carbon-un-idUSL1N0YN08L20150601*

made in "The Profits of Doom," though the companies took the initiative, not the governments.[13]

In his letter written from a Birmingham jail,[14] Martin Luther King Jr. referred to Reinhold Niebuhr and his point that individuals may respond to arguments based on morality and voluntarily yield unjust positions, while groups, including corporations, tend to be less moral than individuals. This point remains generally true, notwithstanding this instance of enlightened action by European oil companies.

The Rev. King and fellow clergy spoke persuasively and repeatedly of a country with racial equality, and accompanied these speeches with confrontations in the form of marches, strikes, boycotts, and sit-ins to exert power against power—those institutions resisting change. Their secular and religious arguments were valid and, in combination with confrontational non-violence, governments eventually enacted laws requiring change and institutions, some more slowly than others, complied.

The heavy use of fossil fuels for our energy needs may be compared to the segregation prevalent in that earlier time. Speeches and books that draw upon scientific and religious arguments for mitigating climate change are needed, but will not succeed in altering our course unless those advocating change also take to the streets. That's the environmental rights movement.

The movement must persuade governments to facilitate the rapid reduction of the use of fossil fuels, and private institutions to alter their energy systems in favor of those less polluting. This may take sit-ins, marches, boycotts, and other forms of protests that demonstrate to governments that a significant percent of the population seeks change and will vote accordingly, and exact a heavy financial and public relations toll on corporations unwilling to modify their energy use, or facilitate a transition out of fossil fuels.

Thus, we need an environmental rights movement with the dual elements employed by Dr. King, persuasion and action. The Rev. Dr. M. L. King's leadership was able to represent both the secular and religious elements of the movement. The environmental rights movement may need to be co-led by a pastor and an environmentalist.

---

13. June 2015 also brought the welcome and encouraging news that global CO_2 emissions from the energy sector were the same in 2014 as in 2013. See, for example, *http://www.climatecentral.org/ news/co2-emissions-stabilized-in-2014-18777* .

14. April 16, 1963. This was an open letter, nominally addressed to eight white clergymen who had asked Dr. King to delay the Birmingham demonstration.

Lest the prospect of sit-ins, marches, and demonstrations sounds discomforting, recall that Jesus was courageous and confrontational. Recall his charge to the apostles:

> "See, I am sending you out like sheep into the midst of wolves; so be wise
> as serpents and innocent as doves."

> Matt. 10:16

Clearly, the fear of opposition did not daunt Jesus, nor did he expect it to affect the work of the apostles.

In the Torah, Moses audaciously confronts the pharaoh of Egypt multiple times asking that he allow the Israelites to leave Egypt. Moses later repeatedly led the Israelites into battles in their campaign to enter the land of Canaan, as God instructed him.

With these examples of confrontation, we should not be timid in pressing for reduced greenhouse gas emissions that so obviously damage creation and whose generation results from actions that violate foundational biblical teachings.

Our demands for change will not, I believe, trigger responses as violent and ugly as those during the civil rights movement. Every summertime electricity brown-out, tornado, fire, and flood will reinforce the message that change is necessary. The earth itself is aiding the cause, painfully so.

15

Environmental Rights Movement: Extended Family

The environmental rights movement may also be helped by numerous existing secular and religious organizations working to reduce greenhouse gas emissions. Those with a religious basis include:

- Evangelical Environmental Network
- Interfaith Power & Light
- National Religious Partnership for the Environment
- Green Faith
- Web of Creation
- The Shalom Center
- North American Coalition for Christianity and Ecology

Initiatives on the secular side that aid an environmental rights movement are, thankfully, too long to list in this chapter, but the tally includes:

- 350.org (*www.350.org*)
  The organization 350.org works to mitigate climate change through "online campaigns, grassroots organizing, and mass public actions" "coordinated by a global network active in over 188 countries."[1] Representative actions have included:

  - Protesting the Keystone XL pipeline that would bring tar sands oil from Canada to Oklahoma and from there to the Gulf of Mexico for export; America's preeminent climatologist James Hansen

---

1. Used with permission.

wrote in 2012 that if the world starts burning oil from the tar sands, it's "game over" for the climate;[2] President Obama denied a permit for the Keystone XL pipeline in November 2015. Tar sands oil continues to be transported by rail and truck, which results in a far slower usage than what the pipeline would have enabled;

- Protesting hydraulic fracturing (fracking) to find natural gas in the Delaware River Basin, an area that provides drinking water for 15 million people; fracking uses enormous amounts of water and runs the risk of contaminating an area's water supply;

- Connecting the Dots: a global demonstration of the connection between climate change and extreme weather;

- Serving as one of the partners that helped organize the People's Climate March in New York City in September 2014, which brought about 400,000 people to the streets of the city demanding an end to a fossil-fuel-based energy system.

- Rainforest Action Network (*www.ran.org*)

Direct action has been a major element of RAN's work throughout its more than forty-year history. RAN expresses its mission as conducting "campaigns for the forest, their inhabitants and the natural systems that sustain life by transforming the global marketplace through education, grassroots organizing and non-violent direct action."[3] RAN has won landmark environmental commitments from corporations such as Citi, Home Depot, Kinko's, Lowe's, and Bank of America.

- The Nature Conservancy (*www.natureconservancy.org*)

The Nature Conservancy purchases and protects ecologically important areas around the world, saving them from loss through development, agriculture, or any other change.

- Natural Resources Defense Council (*www.nrdc.org*)

Legal action is one of the core tools of the NRDC, which works by combining the efforts of its more than one million members with the legal skills of nearly five hundred lawyers, scientists, and other professionals.

---

2. *http://www.nytimes.com/2012/05/10/opinion/game-over-for-the-climate.html?_r=0*

3. Used with permission.

- Environmental Defense Fund (*www.edf.org*)

  EDF characterizes their approach as combining social science, economic incentives, partnerships, and public policy to protect the climate, the oceans, ecosystems, and our health. They have not engaged in either direct action nor courtroom challenges, but use the approaches listed to accomplish the desired changes.

- Sierra Club (*www.sierraclub.org*)

  In 2013, the Sierra Club joined with 350.org in the Forward on Climate rally in Washington, D.C., a gathering that brought together about 40,000 people to urge the Obama administration not to approve the Keystone XL pipeline and to move aggressively on climate change. It was gratifying to see this organization with more than two million members step into this activist role. The Sierra Club claims to have helped retire over 160 coal-fired power plants.

- Earthjustice (*http://earthjustice.org*)

  Earthjustice uses the power of the law to combat climate change, protect human health, and preserve beautiful places and wildlife.

- Architecture 2030 (*www.architecture2030.org*)

  Architecture 2030, founded by the noted New Mexico architect Edward Mazria, introduced the idea that by the year 2030, architects and engineers should design buildings that use no net energy; that is, whatever fossil fuel energy a building will use must be offset by renewable energy generated onsite, for example, by photovoltaic (PV) panels, and/or purchasing (20 percent maximum) renewable energy.[4] Mazria observed that the building sector constitutes the largest contributor to carbon emissions. Perhaps it can also be a major source of carbon reductions.

Professional organizations such as the American Institute of Architects (AIA), the American Society of Heating, Refrigerating, and Air Conditioning Engineers (ASHRAE), and the U.S. Green Building Council (USGBC) adopted this idea, each with slight variations, and offer education and techniques by which their members can reduce the energy requirements of buildings. ASHRAE has taken the commendable steps of (1) stating its belief that zero net energy buildings (ZNEB) constitute a

---

4. *www.architecture2030.org*

realistic goal for 2030, and (2) declaring its intent to provide its members the resources necessary to design and operate ZNEB by 2020.

This concerted effort by building sector professional organizations has proven successful. In a January 2012 e-mail, Architecture 2030 reported that the Energy Information Administration (EIA), part of the U.S. Department of Energy, published its 2011 forecast of U.S. building energy consumption and emissions in 2030. In 2005, the EIA estimated a 53.1 percent increase in CO_2 emissions by 2030, from 2005 levels. The 2011 estimate projects just a 4.6 percent increase and, with the best available technology used, a decrease of 16.5 percent below 2005 levels. This is very good news.

The design profession has clearly made progress in reaching carbon neutrality by 2030, and the suite of tools that enable energy efficient designs are being increasingly adopted by professionals. As more of them do so, the pace of carbon reductions from this sector will increase.

Which brings us to additional good news: CNN (*www.cnn*.com) reported on June 22, 2012, that according to the U.S. Energy Information Administration our energy sector has cut carbon emissions by nine percent since 2007. Overall U.S. greenhouse gas emissions, not just those from the energy sector, dropped 5 percent from 2005 to 2010, and European emissions dropped 9 percent during that period.

This rate of carbon reductions is not yet steep enough to avert the most painful consequences of climate change, but sustained pressure from individuals and organizations can, I believe, get us there.

That is why every voice expressing the insignificance of their individual action is wrong, frustrating, and possibly sinful—an attribute we'll cover shortly. The progress made has resulted from countless actions by governments, corporations, and business owners, as well as from millions of individuals who buy gas-electric hybrid cars,[5] select high efficiency refrigeration and HVAC equipment, install PV arrays on their commercial or residential buildings, and purchase energy efficient products.

---

5. Hybrid cars, rather than all-electric vehicles (EV), are mentioned because hybrids do not require recharging from a source of electricity. When EVs can be charged mainly by low- to non-polluting sources such as natural gas, wind, hydro, or solar power they will offer significant air quality and environmental health benefits over both gasoline-only and gasoline-electric vehicles. (See "Life cycle air quality impacts of conventional and alternative light-duty transportation in the United States," Christopher W. Tessum, Jason D. Hill, and Julian D. Marshall, Proceedings of the National Academy of Sciences of the United States of America, vol. 111, No. 52, Dec. 30, 2014. *www.pnas.org/content/111/52/18490*)

CNN reported,[6] however, that the largest contributor—though not the only one—to reduced greenhouse gas emissions is low natural gas prices arising from a dramatic increase in natural gas production through fracking—a mixed blessing. This process brings risks of contaminating drinking water supplies and of earthquakes, major effects that in 2015 should accelerate the study of the process and slow its rapid growth until study results are concluded.

The inexpensive natural gas has motivated some electricity companies to switch from coal to natural gas for electricity generation, with the change delivering roughly 50 percent reductions in CO_2 emissions. In April of 2012, for the first time since the EIA began keeping records , equal amounts of electricity were generated with natural gas as with coal.[7] The actual climate change benefit of this remains unclear: The methane gas released during fracking has 21 times the global warming potential (GWP) of carbon dioxide; that is, one pound of methane released into the atmosphere has the effect of 21 pounds of CO_2. The gases released during fracking and those emitted during combustion could exceed the global warming potential of a coal operation.[8]

While the switch from coal to natural gas accounts for the largest drop in carbon emissions, with the total greenhouse gas effect still undetermined, one cannot dismiss the reductions arising from changes in the building design profession discussed earlier, nor those coming from individual decisions; they are all part of the solution.

However, indifference, or failure to act to accelerate the rate of greenhouse gas reductions, may also be seen as sinful. The Catholic idea of the seven deadly sins (or capital sins, since they lead to others) refers to a list put into its familiar form by Pope Gregory I in the sixth century, but dates back to the fourth century. One of the deadly sins is *acedia*, a Greek word that identifies the sin as sloth, discouragement, or, in modern terms, the failure to do what one should do. Thus, under Catholic teaching, responses such as "there's not much I can do," or "I don't have the energy for this," or "I think it's hopeless," may be sinful responses to the climate imperative upon us. We are obligated to do what we can to avert this self-inflicted plague upon the planet.

---

6. "U.S. cuts greenhouse gases despite do-nothing Congress," CNN Money, June 21, 2012.

7. From the Energy Information Administration. *http://www.eia.gov/todayinenergy/detail.cfm?id=6990*

8. See also *www.eeb.cornell.edu/howarth/publications/GHG_update_April_11_2011.pdf*

In the Hebrew literature, one of the teachings in *Sayings of the Fathers* (Pirke Avot) includes a similar requirement to act: "You are not required to complete the task, yet you are not free to withdraw from it."[9] Thus, from two quite different perspectives we find the obligation to act when a need has been recognized.

Human beings respond quickly to immediate needs, such as imminent threats to our safety, but do less well with dangers whose consequences are years out. Before the year 1995, to pick one point in time, one could argue that forecasts placing the dire consequences of climate change decades into the future explained our slow response to the crisis. That can no longer serve as an explanation, for the consequences are now upon us. What the planet has experienced in the past decade is equivalent to a "slap upside the head." Consider:

- Fires of historic proportions in Texas in 2011 and Colorado in 2012, and fires striking the states of California, Oregon, Nevada, Washington, and Idaho in August 2012;
- The shrinking of Lake Chad, one of the largest lakes on the planet, from an area of 10,000 square miles to about 500 square miles in less than 40 years. The loss of water, fish, biodiversity, and livelihood affects more than 20 million people in the countries of Chad, Nigeria, Cameroon, and Niger;
- Huge, prolonged rainfalls in the Philippines in August 2012 affecting 850,000 people;
- The average temperature across global land and ocean surfaces in the first three months of 2015 was the highest ever recorded for that period in the 1880–2015 history, and March 2015 had the highest average temperature for that month ever experienced;[10]
- Unprecedented tornado activity in 2010–2012;
- The deadliest wildfires in Australia's history in 2009 that included a fast-moving firestorm that either cut off or outran people trying to escape in their cars; the fires were helped, in part, by a long-running drought and a period of high temperatures;
- Flooding in Pakistan in August–September 2011 that affected 5.5 million people;

9. From Pirke Avot 2:21, *http://ancientwisdom4ustoday.org.*

10. *https://www.ncdc.noaa.gov/sotc/*

- The evacuation of 450,000 people in August 2012 in advance of China's third typhoon in less than a week;
- The ten warmest years on record occurred between 1998 and 2014, with 2014 being the hottest.[11]

These are just a few examples of climate change effects that occurred over years and those that happened suddenly. An increase in the frequency of extreme weather events is one predicted outcome of climate change. As noted earlier, in response to the caveat that no particular extreme event can be linked to climate change, James Hansen stated that "there is virtually no explanation other than climate change."

Many of us, globally, heard the message and want to act to avert a catastrophic collapse of our life-support systems. The good news is that (1) we actually have a pretty good idea of what to do, and (2) we still have time.

The bad news is that in this crucial area the U.S. has acted, until the administration of President Barack Obama, like an anchor weighing down the rest of the world. This country could enable the devastating effects of climate change to engulf the planet, our total CO_2 emissions are so high. An environmental rights movement, a movement that asserts *we have the right to an environment that supports life*, could spur this influential giant.

The anchor was raised significantly during the Obama presidency by White House and EPA announcements of substantive moves to address climate change. The initiatives include:

- New automobile and light-duty truck fuel efficiency standards that will increase fuel economy to the equivalent of 54.5 mpg by model year 2025.[12] The Administration's overall national program to improve fuel economy and reduce greenhouse gas emissions is estimated to reduce oil consumption by more than 2 million barrels a day by 2025. Consumer average gas pump savings over the lifetime of a vehicle are estimated at $8,000 by 2025;
- The refusal to approve the Keystone XL pipeline, whose existence would accelerate the burning of tar sands-based oil that releases about 30 percent more CO_2 into the atmosphere than conventional oil;

---

11. *http://climate.nasa.gov/blog/2224*

12. *www.whitehouse.gov/the-press-office/2012/08/28/obama-administration-finalizes-historic-545-mpg-fuel-efficiency-standard.*

- An end to loans to help construct coal-fired electricity generation plants anywhere in the world. The World Bank announced a similar move in July 2013 saying it would limit financing of coal-fired power plants to "rare circumstances";
- Major reductions in allowable CO_2 emissions from new and existing coal-fired electricity generation plants;
- A November 2014 agreement with China[13] that includes provisions to:

  - Spur the adoption of an agreement with legal force on all applicable parties at the United Nations Conference on Climate Change in Paris in 2015;[14]
  - Reduce U.S. economy-wide emissions by 26–28 percent below the 2005 level by 2025. The President of China agreed to achieve the peaking of CO_2 emissions by 2030 and to increase the share of non-fossil fuels to around 20 percent by 2030.

If these beneficial measures are sustained by future administrations and additional measures are undertaken by the U.S., China, and other countries, the world has a chance to hold atmospheric CO_2 below a level that would devastate our planet for centuries.

---

13. *http://www.whitehouse.gov/the-press-office/2014/11/11/us-china-joint-announcement-climate-change*

14. Though this did not happen, the agreement signed was remarkable and gratifying, for 196 nations concurred that increasing amounts of greenhouse gas emissions are leading to likely devastating and irreversible changes to our planet, and they identified the reductions in such emissions each nation pledged to achieve.

16

Preserving Our Home

Climate change presents this generation—and it is *this* generation[1]—with highly complex environmental and economic problems not previously encountered in human experience. We have dealt with wars, epidemics, earthquakes, and firestorms, but never before have we been required to consider preserving the climate to which we and our ancestors, going back millennia, have become accustomed. Future generations may not have this problem, but the far larger one of adjusting to a planet that year-by-year becomes more inhospitable: more droughts, more diseases, higher temperatures, and less water and food.

In addition, the challenge of climate change is heightened by requiring part of our citizenry to act with urgency on a problem that for others appears distant or nonexistent. Acting with foresight is not something our species tends to do well.

When Pearl Harbor was attacked in 1941, what had been a threat was now a fact and the U.S. responded vigorously. Anyone who advocated America not respond would have been considered to be betraying the country. Similarly, the fires that torched Texas, Colorado, Arizona, and California; the tornados that smashed Missouri, Arkansas, Oklahoma, Alabama, and Mississippi; and Superstorm Sandy and Hurricane Katrina all constitute attacks on our country, not by a foreign power but by the new, hostile climate we are creating. These weather attacks, like bombs and other weapons, also kill people and livestock, and destroy homes, churches, stores, forests, and much more. How often have we heard survivors say that their stricken community now looks like a war zone?

But some among us, a few with great wealth, influence, and a stake in the status quo, urge us to do nothing. That advice seems to me to be a

---

1. Every adult alive in the second decade of the twenty-first century.

betrayal of our country and our planet. To refute scientific data with no counter-analysis, or willingly ignore both the data and the devastation parts of the country have suffered in order to proclaim the threat a fabrication, is an act of betrayal—an act that puts short-term personal profit ahead of the wellbeing of the country. In "World's Greatest Crime against Humanity and Nature," James Hansen asserts a similar perspective.[2]

This book seeks to demonstrate to people of faith that their personal behavior, and that of institutions over which they have some control, have contributed—in some instances unwittingly—to the not-so-slow devastation of God's creation. I believe that this will prove unacceptable, and people of faith will be motivated to push forcefully against the loud, immoral voices that deny data and physical evidence for personal gain.

The single number that best characterizes climate change is the amount of CO_2 in the atmosphere. That figure stands at about 400 ppm in 2015 and will remain at that level or higher for centuries. It is extremely unlikely to decrease. The number of ppm relates directly to the increase in temperature the earth is experiencing relative to the long-term average temperature.

Slowing the damaging effects of climate change—prolonged heat waves, droughts, violent weather events, fires—means reducing increases to the ppm value. We can do that *most quickly* by conserving energy and using renewable and nuclear energy rather than fossil-fuel-based energy. That is why these items are first and second on the list of measures to slow climate change. Each of the entries is discussed further in the sections that follow.

Action Plan to Slow Climate Change[3]

1. Redouble efforts with energy conservation measures in the industrial, commercial, and residential sectors of our society.

2. Continue installations of rooftop solar panels (photovoltaic [PV] systems) and wind turbines to offset fossil-fuel-based electricity with renewable energy.

---

2. James E. Hansen, "World's Greatest Crime against Humanity and Nature," *www.columbia.edu/~jeh1/mailings/2014/20140310_ChinaOpEd.pdf*

3. This list is drawn primarily from the writings of James Hansen and Amory Lovins, two internationally respected figures. Not all measures listed are advocated by both scholars, but at least one of them recommends most of the actions given. Dr. James Hansen is the former director of the NASA Goddard Institute for Space Studies and is now an adjunct professor at the Columbia University Earth Institute. Amory Lovins is the co-founder of the Rocky Mountain Institute (RMI), chief scientist, and chairman emeritus.

3. Close coal-fired electricity generating plants, either shutting them down or converting them to natural gas for the near term.

4. Begin the construction of third generation nuclear plants to meet our substantial, long-term demand for electricity with a stable, CO_2-free energy source. While a contentious recommendation for some, the design of this new generation of nuclear plants gives them the ability to shut down passively and cool the core in case an accident disrupts all electrical power.[4]

5. Reduce emissions of non-CO_2 greenhouse gases that contribute to climate change, such as methane, nitrous oxide, and hydrofluorocarbons.

6. Enact a carbon fee or price on carbon to provide an economic incentive for energy providers and the public to move away from the use of fossil fuels.

7. Transform the transportation sector from one that relies on steel and aluminum for vehicle bodies, for example, hood, trunk, doors, to one that uses lighter, stronger, and safer carbon fiber.

8. Engage in a world-wide reforestation project to capture large amounts of CO_2. Hansen recommends capturing 100 gigatons of carbon (GtC) within fifty years.

9. Conduct research on fourth generation nuclear plants. In addition to the safety feature of passive cooling with third generation plants, these have the ability to "burn" the spent fuel from second and third generation plants. This would solve the problem of nuclear waste disposal.

10. Shut down all coal and oil electricity plants as third generation reactors come on line, and then close natural gas plants as fourth generation plants become operational and the replacement capacity allows.

Items 1–9 are meant to run in parallel; that is, to continue or to start immediately, with item 10 occurring later.

This plan is offered, first, as an attempt to answer succinctly the oft-repeated question, "What can we really do about climate change?" Some books with a religious bent, like this one, appear to suggest that if people lived in accord with biblical teachings, the climate change problem would be solved. Living in accord with the environmental teachings in the Pentateuch would benefit our planet and strengthen our connection to the

---

4. *http://www.world-nuclear.org/info/Nuclear-Fuel-Cycle/Power-Reactors/Advanced-Nuclear-Power-Reactors/*

Divine. Sadly, however, it would not solve the current climate change problem. This might be true if we had lived differently since the industrial revolution, but not given the dismal status quo. Instead, a major transformation of the way the U.S. provides energy is needed, in addition to individual measures, energy conservation, and the use of renewables. Second, the plan offers to members of an environmental rights movement individual actions around which to mobilize.

Some observations about each of the plan's ten elements:

Item 1—Redouble efforts with energy conservation

It is not a joke to say that the plug from a television set, in all likelihood, ultimately connects to a fossil-fuel-based power plant. Every hour the TV is off, less CO_2 enters the atmosphere. Researchers for years have been promoting the benefits of energy conservation, for the practice avoids emissions and yields cost savings.

We, the people, can drive change in this country—and we must, for apathy or self-indulgence will cause us more pain each passing year. If we purchase hybrid cars rather than gas-only models, automobile manufacturers will respond by making more hybrid cars and fewer gas-only ones: they won't make products that don't sell. And we can bring about that change faster than with government intervention, important as that sometimes is. By our decisions, we drive change.

More than 134.5 million cars cruise America's roadways.[5] If gas consumption dropped by just one gallon per month per car, CO_2 emissions would drop by 14.4 million metric tons (Mmt) per year.[6] That's not trivial for a single measure.

We live in more than 98 million homes and 34.3 million apartments.[7] If we turned off a single 100 Watt appliance for two hours per day, we would cut CO_2 emissions by more than 6.6 Mmt per year. Again, that's not trivial for a single measure.

Individuals in the residential sector can conserve energy in many ways, most of them familiar by now. These include: Avoid idling of cars, trucks, and buses; turn off TVs, appliances, and lights when they are not in use; carpool to work, saving you money and preventing emissions of greenhouse

---

5. http://www.statista.com/statistics/192998/registered-passenger-cars-in-the-united-states-since-1975/

6. www2.epa.gov/energy/greenhouse-gas-equivalencies-calculator

7. http://quickfacts.census.gov/qfd/states/00000.html

gases; and purchase energy-efficient equipment, for that will often have the lowest cost over the lifetime of the product.

Further energy conserving opportunities and resources for the residential sector are discussed in Part III.

The power of the individual to slow climate change extends to advocacy as well. Collectively, we can pressure utilities to convert to non-CO_2 emitting electricity generation; pressure car, bus, and truck companies to use carbon fiber for vehicle bodies; and pressure appliance manufacturers to improve the energy efficiency of their products. We will return to the crucial role of advocacy and an environmental rights movement in chapters 17–18.

For the commercial and industrial sectors, *Reinventing Fire*[8] includes a number of recommendations for the building sector, for transportation, and for industry.

Energy conservation efforts achieved impressive savings with both commercial and residential buildings between 1980 and 2000, with the average commercial building energy use per square foot dropping by about 20 percent and the average residential building energy use per square foot falling by about one-third. Much more can be done, however, with proven technologies such as high efficiency lighting (for example, LED lighting), efficient motors, pumps, fans, and piping designs, and covers for refrigerated cases in supermarkets.[9]

The diversity of the transportation sector—for example, cars, trucks, buses, and airplanes—provides numerous opportunities to reduce fuel usage, and thereby emissions, with perhaps the most effective one coming from reducing a vehicle's weight. Huge fuel savings could be attained by the widespread use of carbon fiber.

A carbon fiber hood, for example, is stronger and weighs less than a steel or aluminum one. A wholesale switch to carbon fiber for vehicle bodies would save significant amounts of fuel. This topic is covered further in Item 7.

Hybrid cars are driving up overall fuel efficiency in the automobile sector; additional measures worth exploring include tires with low rolling resistance, reduced drag coefficients through improved vehicle design, and non-CO_2 polluting fuel cells for propulsion.[10]

---

8. *Reinventing Fire: Bold Business Solutions for the New Energy Era,* Amory B. Lovins and Rocky Mountain Institute, Chelsea Green Publishing, White River Junction, Vermont, 2011.

9. Lovins, *Reinventing Fire*, chapter 3.

10. Lovins, *Reinventing Fire*, chapter 2.

The Clinton, Bush, and Obama administrations helped support the development of fuel-cell technology, in part because cars and other types of transportation account for about 28 percent of U.S. greenhouse gas emissions, according to the EPA. Only water and heat come from the tailpipe of hydrogen fuel-cell vehicles.

Toyota, with the Mirai, and Hyundai, with the Tucson, began marketing their fuel-cell cars in California in 2015, because the state is rapidly building a refueling infrastructure. General Motors, Ford, Audi and other companies are reportedly working on similar vehicles. This constitutes a genuine and heartening transformation of the automobile market—the availability of cars that release no greenhouse gas emissions and do not require either gasoline or electricity for refueling.

While great diversity exists in the industrial sector, a few energy-saving measures having broad applicability include: using the most efficient motors, pumps, and fans, and turning off motors when not in use; increasing the use of combined heat and power (CHP) in America's factories; and in data centers using the most efficient servers, using outside air for free cooling when the temperature and humidity allow, and replacing uninterruptible power supplies with on-site ultra-reliable fuel cells with heating and cooling as byproducts.[11]

Many corporations have benefited from implementing energy saving measures, and a few major examples include the carpet manufacturer Interface, Dow, United Technologies, and 3M. Interface benefited dramatically, for over a sixteen-year period the founder of the company, the late Ray C. Anderson, enabled eight of its nine manufacturing plants to operate on 100 percent renewable energy, reduced energy use per unit of product by 43 percent, and lowered waste costs by 42 percent, saving $438 million.[12]

Retailers such as JC Penney, Staples, and Kohl's and supermarkets such as Food Lion, Kroger, Albertson's, and The Great Atlantic & Pacific Tea Company each have large numbers of stores recognized by EPA's ENERGY STAR program as among the top 25 percent in energy efficiency compared to comparable stores.

Every competitor of Interface, Dow, United Technologies, 3M, and the retail and supermarket companies listed knows that it too must reduce

---

11. Lovins, *Reinventing Fire*, chapter 4.
12. Lovins, *Reinventing Fire*, chapter 4.

operating costs to stay competitive, and energy improvement represents one strategy that benefits both them and the environment.

Item 2—Continue installations of rooftop solar panels (photovoltaic [PV] systems) and wind turbines

The generation of electricity by solar PV panels and wind turbines avoids CO_2 emissions. Installations of such facilities should continue, though considerations should be given to the different operating characteristics and indirect effects of such renewable energy systems.

- Solar panels on homes and businesses provide electricity without CO_2 emissions and reduce the owner's electricity costs. The reduction of costs can come from both the lack of charges for the solar-provided electricity and a bill credit for the electricity sent to the grid when it is not needed on site.
- The output from solar systems is often well correlated with times of peak demand on utility company systems, and therefore these installations can reduce the likelihood of brownouts or blackouts.
- Wind power has the advantage of flexibility, compared to nuclear and fossil fuel plants, for it can be shut down or turned back on reasonably quickly.
- Nominal wind power availability changes on a monthly basis, with some U.S. locations yielding significantly less output during high demand summer months. A report from The NorthBridge Group includes the finding that in three regions of the country, on the ten peak demand days of the year, more than 80 percent of designed wind capacity was not operating.[13] This observation is supported by data from the Energy Information Administration that reveals available wind energy by month in five locations: Texas; California; Iowa; Illinois; and Minnesota. In four of the five locations, California the exception, wind power output drops to its lowest levels during July–September.[14]

---

13. Frank Huntowski, Aaron Patterson, and Michael Schnitzer, "Negative Electricity Prices and the Production Tax Credit," The NorthBridge Group, September 14, 2012.

14. "Electric Power Monthly Report," U.S. Department of Energy, Energy Information Administration, March 4, 2015. For a graphical presentation of this data, see *http://en.wikipedia.org/wiki/Wind_power_in_the_United_States#statistics.*

However, considering centralized renewable energy plants as the *backbone* of a post-fossil fuel system may prove risky. Climate *change* is the instigator of these efforts, and ten to twenty years from now locations that historically have been good for solar and wind may have less favorable characteristics. That is, we may have more cloudy skies where we have usually had clear ones, and areas with high winds may have become calmer. These possibilities may appear remote, but they might serve as another reason to consider a non-climate-dependent technology, such as nuclear energy, as the major replacement for our fossil fuel systems.

Distributed PV systems, however, can provide a continuously increasing amount of the electricity needed in homes and businesses, and with advanced battery storage may be able to meet some or all of the nighttime needs as well. This prospect moved closer to reality with the encouraging announcement in April 2015 by Tesla Motors of their Powerwall system.[15] This 7-kW or 10-kW wall-mountable battery pack, which is scalable, can be charged during the day by a roof-mounted PV array and then provide electricity at night. This could have a profound effect on the attractiveness of solar energy systems.

Item 3—Close coal-fired electricity generating plants

Producing electricity through the burning of coal is destructive to the environment from the beginning of the process to the end. Just the act of blasting the tops off mountains to mine for coal violates nature and is incompatible with the goal of using the land "in ways commensurate with the holiness of its owner." Besides the desecration of the landscape, the process sends tons of dirt and rock into the land and waters below. The EPA estimates that 2,000 miles of Appalachian headwater streams have been buried by strip mining through mountain-top removal.[16]

Transporting coal in long freight trains with uncovered cars sends coal dust into the land, air, and water of all communities through which the trains pass. Coal plants typically draw water from nearby lakes, rivers, or oceans and, depending upon the cooling system type, may consume around one billion gallons of water each year of the total water withdrawn.

Coal-burning electricity plants constitute the largest stationery source of CO_2 emissions. In 2013, coal-burning plants sent about 1,720 million

---

15. See *www.teslamotors.com/powerwall*

16. Union of Concerned Scientists: *www.ucsusa.org/clean_energy/our-energy-choices/energy-and-water-use/water-energy-electricity-coal.html*

metric tons of CO_2 into the atmosphere,[17] which is about 30 percent of total U.S. CO_2 emissions.

The burning of coal creates tons of coal ash and sludge waste that includes toxins such as mercury, arsenic, chromium, and cadmium. A 600-MW coal plant would produce about 125,000 tons of ash and 190,000 tons of sludge each year. About 39,000 tons of coal ash and 27,000 gallons of contaminated water leaked from a Duke Energy storage pool into the Dan River in 2014.[18] Contaminants spilling into a river damage its entire ecosystem and ultimately harm those who consume the water and fish from the river. A 2008 breach of a coal ash waste dike associated with a TVA plant dumped an estimated 1.1 billion gallon mix of coal ash and water into the Emory River in Tennessee.[19]

About 60,000 cancer cases have been linked to just mountain-top removal for coal,[20] and the U.N. has estimated a global toll of one million deaths annually due to fossil fuel air and water pollution.[21] Generating electricity by burning coal has deadly and devastating consequences that we must end, for multiple reasons, by transitioning to non-polluting forms of electricity generation.

Item 4—Begin the construction of third generation nuclear plants

The U.S. operates what are termed second generation nuclear reactors, those developed after the installation of the earliest nuclear-powered electricity generating facilities. Some third generation nuclear plants are operating in a few countries, for example, Japan, but in the U.S. most remain under construction.

This recommendation from James Hansen[22] to construct third generation nuclear plants will likely prove contentious initially, and it does

17. U.S. Energy Information Administration, April 2014 Monthly Energy Review, Table 12.1: Carbon Dioxide Emissions from Energy Consumption by Source.

18. *http://thinkprogress.org/climate/2014/04/01/3421513/duke-begins-clean-up-dan-river/*

19. Union of Concerned Scientists: *www.ucsusa.org/clean_energy/our-energy-choices/energy-and-water-use/water-energy-electricity-coal.html*

20. James Hansen, "Baby Lauren and the Kool-Aid," p. 7, citing an article in the Huffington Post: *www.huffingtonpost.com/jeff-biggers/breaking-new-study-links-b_910739.html*

21. James Hansen, "The Case for Young People and Nature: A Path to a Healthy, Natural, Prosperous Future, p. 2, referencing Cohen et al, 2005: "The global burden of disease due to outdoor air pollution," *J. Toxicol. Environ. Health*, 68, 1301–7, doi:1080/152873905909361666.

22. James Jansen, "World's Greatest Crime against Humanity," *www.columbia.edu/~jeh1/mailings/2014/20140310_ChinaOpEd.pdf.*

represent a turnaround for me personally. I was opposed to nuclear power for two main reasons: (1) the danger of a nuclear meltdown if the core could not be cooled due to loss of electrical power; and (2) the inability to dispose of, or safely store, nuclear waste with a half-life measured in millennia.

But third and fourth generation nuclear plants remove these objections: third and fourth generation plants have cooling systems that can passively shut down and lower the temperature of the core without operator intervention or electrical power, and fourth generation plants utilize about 99 percent of their nuclear fuel, leaving a small amount in waste that has a half-life measured in centuries, not millennia. These plants can also "burn" nuclear waste from second and third generation plants, from depleted uranium, and from excess weapons material. Stockpiles from these latter materials contain enough fuel to power fourth generation reactors for centuries, ending the need to mine for uranium. Thus, third and fourth generation plants appear to solve the nuclear meltdown concern, and fourth generation plants resolve the nuclear waste issue.

In addition to these features that address safety and storage concerns, nuclear reactors are logical choices to replace coal, oil, and gas electricity generation plants for strong technical reasons: All four are, ultimately, synchronous rotary machines; that is, they are mechanical generators with rotating shafts synchronized to the electrical frequency of the grid. Indeed, according to Graham Palmer, 96 percent of global electricity is generated by such machines. [23]

Synchronous generation is integral to the mechanism for grid control, that is, ensuring that electricity generation matches demand at every moment. Wind turbines and solar PV systems are examples of non-synchronous generators. Their output can vary from moment to moment due to variations in wind speed and cloud cover, respectively. In addition, the output from solar PV panels ends during nighttime hours, if no electricity from a storage system is available.

Integrating electricity generated from non-synchronous generators into a system dominated by synchronous generators is complex and, to a degree, destabilizing. Thus, closing coal-fired, synchronous generation plants and replacing their capacity with nuclear plants is relatively straightforward. Replacing coal plants with solar or wind power is not straightforward. A

---

23. Graham Palmer, *Energy in Australia: Peak Oil, Solar Power, and Asia's Economic Growth* (New York: Springer, 2014), 17.

full discussion of this is beyond the scope of this book, but the slim volume by Palmer provides an excellent description.

Another compelling reason for favoring nuclear technology over a large scale solar plant lies in its high output and efficient use of land. The Ivanpah solar thermal power system is a concentrating solar power plant that began operation in 2013.[24] It consists of over 300,000 software-controlled mirrors that track the sunlight and reflect it to boilers that sit atop three 459-foot towers. The boilers heat water to create high-temperature steam, which is then piped to standard turbines. These, in turn, generate electricity. The reflected sunlight, however, can burn/vaporize birds that fly in its path. Estimates of bird kills range from 1,000 to 28,000 per year, with recent investigators reporting an average of one bird kill every two minutes.[25] Officials from the U.S. Fish and Wildlife Service have requested a tally of the number of bird deaths during a full year of operation.

The Ivanpah site in California, close to the Nevada border, occupies 3,500 acres, or about 5.5 square miles, and provides about 0.8 TWh of electricity per year, according to Hansen's estimates; 1 Terawatt hour, TWh, is 1,000 Gigawatt hours. Ivanpah does not have any storage capacity, requiring another facility to provide electricity at night.

In contrast, Hansen identifies the Westinghouse AP-1000 nuclear plant that requires about 0.5 square miles of land and provides 8.8 TWh each year. Ten Ivanpahs, covering 50 square miles, would be required to yield as much electricity as a single nuclear plant covering 0.5 square miles. This output of 0.8 TWh per 5 square miles may change if the High Concentration Photo Voltaic Thermal (HCPVT) system announced by IBM becomes operational.[26] The HCPVT system is reported to convert 80 percent of the incoming solar radiation into useful energy, far exceeding the current peak conversion efficiency of 44.7 percent.[27] Of course, this would not change the bird kill problem.

The U.S. could begin constructing third generation nuclear plants on existing nuclear plant sites with capacity to accommodate another reactor,

---

24. Ivanpah Project Facts from BrightSource Energy.

25. *http://www.dispatch.com/content/stories/national_world/2014/08/24/rays-from-solar-power-plant-ignite-birds-in-midair.html*

26. *www.collective-evolution.com/2014/02/21/up-for-grabs-ibm-solar-collector-magnifies-sun-2000x/* See also "IBM developing an 80 percent efficient solar power collector," posted April 24, 2013 by MB-BigB, *www.alt-energy.info/author/admin/*.

27. *www.computerworld.com/s/article/9246558/IBM_solar_energy_tech_claims_to_harness_power_of_2_000_suns*, February 24, 2014.

if they exist, and on land occupied by shuttered coal plants; both of these would contain some elements of the needed infrastructure that would reduce construction time and costs.

Item 5—Reduce emissions of non-CO_2 greenhouse gases

Several gases other than CO_2 contribute to climate change, including methane, nitrous oxide, and hydrofluorcarbons. While the amount of each emitted per year is less than CO_2, the global warming potential (GWP) can be higher. The EPA, following an international agreement, identifies the global warming potential for methane as 21 and for nitrous oxide as 310. That means that one pound of nitrous oxide has the effect of 310 pounds of CO_2.

Sources of methane emissions include leakage during production, storage, and transmission; the release of the gas by our food animals, such as cattle, sheep, and goats; and leakage from landfills as waste decomposes.

Nitrous oxide emissions occur when nitrogen is added to the soil through the use of synthetic fertilizers or when motor fuels are burned in cars and trucks.

Hydrofluorocarbons are key components of refrigerants, aerosol propellants, and fire retardants and vent into the atmosphere through leaks when servicing and disposing of such products.[28]

Item 6—Enact a carbon fee or price on carbon

This proposal by James Hansen[29] envisions a fee proportional to the calculated greenhouse gas emissions from the coal, oil, or gas being acquired, with the fee increasing each year. Hansen proposes that the fee "should be collected from fossil fuel companies" at the first point of sale, for example, the mine, oil well, or port of entry. The proposal recommends that the entire amount of the money collected be distributed to households on a monthly basis, thus offsetting cost increases at the retail level. Hansen estimates that 60 percent of us would receive more money from the disbursement than it would cost us for the higher-priced energy. What makes this proposal attractive is that it requires a minimal financial structure, for all money collected "should be distributed electronically each month to bank accounts or debit cards of all legal residents."

---

28. *http://epa.gov/climatechange/ghgemissions/gases/fgases.html*

29. "Baby Lauren and the Kool-Aid," *http://www.columbia.edu/~jeh1/mailings/2011/20110729_BabyLauren.pdf*

As a result of this price on carbon and its disbursements, as well as retail energy price increases, Hansen anticipates energy companies moving to non-fossil fuel technologies and the public making changes in energy choices.

One advantage of a carbon fee, he contends, is that it can readily be made global. An agreement on a price on carbon among a few of the largest economies (U.S., China, European Union, Japan), coupled with border duties on products from countries without a carbon fee, would provide an incentive for the fee to go global.

This point counters another recurring argument that the U.S. should do nothing without an agreement with India and China on reducing emissions. This seems like a "cut off your nose to spite your face" perspective. Moreover, countries reach agreements not solely through negotiations, but with the addition of economic pressures, for example.

Prospects for a price on carbon improved dramatically and surprisingly in June 2015 when six European oil company executives *requested* such a fee in a letter to U.N. climate change leaders preparing for the meeting in Paris in December.[30] The chief executives of BG Group, BP, Eni, Royal Dutch Shell, Statoil, and France's Total wrote that they need governments to provide them with "clear, stable, long-term, ambitious policy frameworks." These would "reduce uncertainty and help stimulate investments in the right low carbon technologies." The letter acknowledged the realization that continued increases in atmospheric CO_2 are not sustainable. American companies such as ExxonMobil and Chevron did not join this request, but perhaps pressure from their European counterparts and the American public will bring them on board.

Congressman John Larson of Connecticut introduced such a bill, called "America's Security Trust Fund Act of 2009." It calls for a fee of $15/ton of CO_2 the first year, increasing by $10/ton per year to $115/ton after ten years. Hansen writes that economic models predict a 30 percent reduction of carbon emissions at the end of ten years which, he believes, would put us on a path to phasing out fossil fuel use by 2050.

Recall that almost complete agreement exists within the climate scientist community that continuing our current use of fossil fuels will subject life on this planet to extreme storms, higher temperatures, more insect-borne diseases, more frequent droughts, floods, and fires, and reduced availability of food and water. Accordingly, this generation—and it is *this*

---

30. *http://www.scribd.com/doc/267327870/Paying-for-Carbon-Letter*

generation—has a choice: We can enact minimally disruptive policies that act to preserve the climate to which life on earth has accommodated over millennia, or we can let ourselves be persuaded by merchants of greed and denial to do nothing and thereby launch ourselves into the increasingly intolerable future described above. Let us "choose life." (Deut. 30:19)

Item 7—Transform the transportation sector through the widespread use of carbon fiber

In an amazing twist, carbon, a central problem when bound in the molecule CO_2, can become part of the solution to climate change when shaped into carbon fiber to replace heavier materials such as steel and aluminum.[31] The use of carbon fiber rather than steel for cars, trucks, planes, and trains would significantly reduce their weight; Lovins estimates that an automobile's weight accounts for more than two-thirds of the energy needed to move it and that, at most, 0.5 percent of the fuel's energy actually moves the driver. Reducing a car's weight with carbon fiber yields the additional benefit of enabling a smaller engine to power the car, thereby further lowering gasoline use and emissions.

More to the point, the Boeing 787 Dreamliner[32] is largely made of a carbon fiber composite, making it one of the most fuel efficient and least polluting aircraft per passenger mile. The paradigm shift in commercial aircraft construction has been demonstrated. It could take decades until most aircraft employ carbon fiber and many years until cars, trucks, buses, and trains also make the switch. But feasibility is no longer in doubt. The question is whether a sufficient number of people who understand the urgency of accelerating this shift can drive its implementation.

The manufacture of a particular product using carbon fiber is a complex process involving two major steps: the production of the carbon fiber itself, on spools or sheets, by one of several processes and the "weaving" of the carbon fibers into a shape that can be hardened with an epoxy or resin into the form needed, such as an airplane fuselage, an automobile hood, or a high-performance bicycle. Step one results in what the industry calls a precursor material, which depends, primarily, on the raw material used. Most of the raw material for carbon fiber now comes from polyacrylonitrile (PAN),

---

31. For example, a carbon fiber hood for a 2013 Chrysler 300C weighs less than half that of the standard model. illstreet: *www.carbonfiberhoods.biz/carbon-fiber-hood-benefits*

32. *www.boeing.com/commercial/787/*

a product that begins development by extracting propylene during the refining of crude oil. The widespread use of carbon fiber is impeded, to a degree, by the longer time needed to fabricate a part compared to current methods.

Some carbon fiber is produced using a lignin precursor, which avoids the use of oil. The lignin is derived from trees or plant material.

Research is underway to produce precursor materials, suitable to production of carbon fiber, derived from coal using chemical processes.[33] This means, among other things, that the coal industry would have a market for its product that did not result in burning the coal and emitting CO_2. Accelerating the development of a coal-based precursor, perhaps with university, industry, and government support, would provide the triple benefits of speeding the transition to carbon fiber and thereby dramatically lowering greenhouse gas emissions, minimizing the use of petroleum-based precursors, and strengthening the coal industry. The commercial viability of this process is a key part of the technology receiving widespread adoption. If this research and technology comes to fruition, the coal industry should face improved prospects for long-term viability and intense pressure from the public to transform mining and transportation into more environmentally sensitive operations, for example, cease blasting the tops off mountains.

In addition, locating new carbon fiber manufacturing plants in states with coal mining operations would reduce transportation costs and bring new industries and employment opportunities to those regions.

Item 8—Engage in a worldwide reforestation project

The millions of acres of trees cut down each year account for about 20 percent of the increase in CO_2 from its preindustrial level, with fossil fuels accounting for 80 percent of the increase, according to James Hansen.[34] A reasonable possibility exists that reforestation and soil storage could play a significant role in drawing down CO_2, with Hansen advocating a

---

33. The research is taking place within industry and in collaboration at the University of Tennessee Space Institute and the center for Advanced Scientific Support and Engineering Technology Company (ASSET.TN).

34. "Scientific Case for Avoiding Dangerous Climate Change to Protect Young People and Nature," James Hansen, Pushker Kharecha, Makiko Sate, Frank Ackerman, Paul J. Hearty, Ove Hoegh-Guldberg, Shi-Ling Hsu, Fred Krueger, Camille Parmesan, Stefan Rahmstorf, Johan Rockstrom, Eelco J. Rohling, Jeffrey Sachs, Pete Smith, Konrad Steffen, Lise Van Susteren, Karina von Schuckmann, James C. Zachos, *www.ourchildrenstrust.org/sites/default/files/Hansen%20et%20al%20 2.16.12.pdf.*

sequestration[35] target of 100 gigatons of carbon (GtC), based on this figure as a rough estimate of the net deforestation to date. Hansen urges sequestering 100 GtC by these two means over a fifty-year period, or an average of 2 GtC per year.

The following discussion constitutes only a "back of the envelope" estimate of carbon sequestration by those two methods. Soil storage of carbon through conservation tillage, cover cropping, and thoughtful crop rotation[36] could capture 0.4–1.2 GtC per year, according to Dr. Rattan Lal, an internationally recognized expert in soil science.[37] Because soil carbon is generally measured in the top 15–30 centimeters, some researchers suspect Lal's estimate could be low because in land with deep-rooted grasses the soil can extend down five meters or more.[38] Nevertheless, it appears we can reach at least half our goal by assuming that the recommended soil storage practices yield a sequestration rate of 1 GtC per year for fifty years. We then look to reforestation to yield the other 1 GtC per year, or 50 GtC over fifty years.

An EPA calculator on greenhouse gas equivalencies[39] indicates that 30.1 acres of forest could sequester 10 metric tons of carbon each year. The sequestration rate depends upon many factors, including the types and ages of trees and the temperature and amount of rainfall. Thus, reforestation in Brazil, Indonesia, and the Congo, as examples, are likely to result in different sequestration rates than in the U.S. If we use the EPA figure, however, and assume a global reforestation rate of 10 million acres of forest per year for 50 years, the total amount of carbon sequestered would reach 4.2 GtC. This does not yield the 50 GtC desired, though constituting a significant contribution. This suggests that we attempt to refine our "rough estimate" of 100 GtC as the net deforestation to date and to maximize the amount of carbon taken up by soil storage.

Global net forest loss between 2000 and 2012 was about 371 million acres.[40] Brazil, which had one of the highest rates of deforestation, steadily

---

35. Carbon sequestration is the long-term storage of carbon in soils, trees and other vegetation, and oceans.

36. Ecological Society of America: *www.esa.org/esa/wp-content/uploads/2012/12/carbonsequestrationinsoils.pdf*

37. R. Lal, "Soil Carbon Sequestration Impacts on Global Climate Change and Food Security," *Science*, Vol. 304, June 11, 2004.

38. Judith D. Schwartz, "Soil as Carbon Storehouse: New Weapon in Climate Fight?" *http://e360.yale.edu/feature/soil_as_carbon_storehouse_new_weapon_in_climate_fight/2744/*, March 2014.

39. See *http://www.epa.gov/cleanenergy/energy-resources/calculator.html#results.*

40. *http://www.bbc.com/news/science-environment-26287137*

reduced the rate between 2005 and 2012. This led to a remarkable drop in the country's greenhouse gas emissions of about 39 percent between 2005 and 2010. Brazil increased deforestation in 2013 and then markedly increased it in 2014. Indonesia, in contrast, continues its high rate of deforestation. In particular, Indonesia is reported to have lost 2,076,000 acres of forest in 2012, while Brazil lost 1,137,000 acres.[41]

Two international agreements in 2013 provide hope for a steady, monitored decrease in deforestation.[42] One came from a U.N. meeting in Warsaw where several developed nations agreed to a group of measures that will provide "results-based" payments to developing nations that reduce carbon emissions by leaving trees standing. A second encouraging step occurred when ten central African countries agreed to protect the Congo Basin rainforest—the world's second largest—through forest monitoring and improved regional cooperation. The monitoring will involve both on-site inspections and remote sensing.

Wildland fires in the U.S. from 1997–2013 burned over 33 million acres,[43] with the fires in the five-year period 2009–2013 affecting over 11 million acres. If the U.S. committed to reforesting that area over the next few decades and Indonesia, Latin American, and African countries each made substantial commitments to reforest tens of millions of acres over several decades, we could approach our goal, assuming willful deforestation goes to zero by 2030 and soil storage contributes more than half that amount. Carbon sequestration by reforestation and soil storage, however, does constitute a benign and low-cost way to help slow climate change.

Another encouraging step occurred at the Lima Climate Change Conference of December 2014. Eight Latin American countries agreed to replant 20 million hectares (49 million acres) of degraded land by the year 2020. A notable and encouraging aspect of this plan is that it will be financed not by charities or governments but by five private investment funds that have committed a total of $365 million, with the Luxemburg-based Althelia Climate Fund making the largest contribution.[44]

41. http://www.theguardian.com/environment/2014/jun/29/rate-of-deforestation-in-indonesia-over takes-brazil-says-study

42. http://www.bbc.com/news/science-environment-25060843

43. Historically significant wildland fires, 1997–2013, www.nifc.gov/fireInfo/fireInfo_stats-lg-Fires.html.

44. "Mexico will replant 8.5 million hectares," http://mexiconewsdaily.com/news/mexico-will-replant-8-5-ha-forestry-plan/, December 9, 2014.

Item 9—Conduct research on fourth generation nuclear plants

The term "fourth generation reactors" denotes three types of advanced thermal reactors and three types of fast reactors. None of these operate now, though China began construction on one type of thermal reactor in 2012 that it plans to have operational in 2017.[45] Most of the other reactors in the design and development phases will not be operational until about 2030.

A thermal reactor uses a neutron moderator to slow the neutrons emitted by fission in order to make them more likely to be captured by the fuel.

A fast reactor is designed to "burn" some of the waste products, called actinides, in order to further reduce waste and to "breed more fuel." Such reactors offer significant advances in safety, economics, and proliferation resistance (at least theoretically).

One type of fast reactor, in which Bill Gates, of Microsoft, is apparently involved, is called a traveling wave reactor (TWR).[46] While most fast reactors require that depleted uranium be taken to a special facility for enrichment or chemical separation before returning to the reactor as an additional source of fuel, a TWR accomplishes the enrichment within the core. This greatly enhances proliferation resistance and offers cost advantages as well. The core of a traveling wave reactor is designed to remain closed for about forty years. Companies involved in fourth generation reactors include TerraPower, General Atomic, Areva, and Westinghouse.

Item 10—Shut down fossil fuel electricity generating plants as third and fourth generation nuclear plants become operational

The U.S. and the rest of the world must end the use of fossil fuels if we hope to preserve a livable planet. Electricity generation constitutes a major source of greenhouse gas emissions, calling us to phase out large fossil fuel generation facilities as large scale nuclear plants become available. Renewable energy will continue to play a significant role, but large synchronous fossil fuel generators require replacement, I believe, by large synchronous nuclear generators. Besides preserving a hospitable environment by avoiding CO_2 emissions, the transition can deliver significant cost savings by

---

45. *www.china.org.cn/business/2013-01/06/content_27606925.htm*

46. *http://terrapower.com/*

ending the mining and drilling for coal, oil, and gas and their transport, sometimes hazardous, over large distances.

It can be emotionally taxing to live at a time of societal transformation and global shifts. Episodes of wars and epidemics exemplify such times, and surviving them means trying to deal with the losses they cause and return to the pre-disaster period. As we've noted, as resources of food and energy become more limited as a result of ongoing climate change, increasing periods of war and epidemics may be a consequence.

The transformation from fossil fuels to renewables and nuclear energy happily do not require combat or disease and their associated losses, nor returning to an earlier epoch. Rather, the shift will improve the health of all and yield a society able to develop with ample, low-cost energy to power advancement.

The transformation will cause major shifts in employment and industries, but I believe governments at all levels can help the society navigate through these. We do so when required by wars and epidemics, and we have the ability to do so under benign conditions. We just need the will.

Part III

A Call to Action—Local Level

17

The Carbon Fiber Revolution

The use of carbon fiber in place of aluminum and steel in ground and air transportation vehicles substantially reduces their weight, without any compromise in strength, and consequently reduces the fuel needed to move from one point to another. Carbon fiber constitutes one key technology by which our country can lower its use of fuel oil and, consequently, CO_2 emissions. Autos, buses, and trucks built with carbon fiber can be powered by smaller engines with no drop in performance.

What can an individual do to accelerate the use of carbon fiber? Plenty! A single individual can press an issue with a car manufacturer or join an existing local nonprofit. Or, a group of like-minded friends can launch an initiative, or start an online petition, or act in concert with a national organization that is pushing the issue you find compelling. The actions involve advocacy, rather than personal measures, and involve both the supply and demand side of the issue.

On the supply side, the goal is to establish carbon fiber manufacturing plants, preferably near coal-mining operations. Advocates of this can:

- Urge the creation of partnerships among universities, coal companies, and government to speed the development of carbon fiber from coal using a chemical process, that is, a method that avoids the burning of coal. This is a necessary first step for an acceptable fiber derived from coal. Until accomplished, carbon fiber applications can be accelerated using polyacrylonitrile (PAN) as the precursor material.

- Contact executives of coal companies to urge that they diversify into carbon fiber manufacturing, in part to blunt the effects of less coal for electricity generation.[1] The coal industry is undergoing major

---

1. In 2014, the amount of electricity (kilowatt hours) generated by coal-fired power plants was 39 percent, down significantly from its 1990–2010 annual average of about 50 percent. *http://www.eia. gov/tools/faqs/faq.cfm?id=427&t=3. http://www.eia.gov/todayinenergy/detail.cfm?id=8450.*

changes, which affect jobs and company profits; fighting those changes by urging the continued burning of coal for electricity generation is a backward-looking and deadly strategy. Rather, state governments and the federal government must acknowledge the transformation underway, and help miners maintain an income while preparing and obtaining alternate work and help the companies maintain their viability while accomplishing the required transition;

- Urge the state secretaries of commerce (and the governors) to support that effort. Benefits to the states include a new industry and new jobs;

- Urge executives of existing carbon fiber manufacturing operations to increase production capacity using PAN. Also urge the executives to open a plant near a coal-mining operation, when a coal-based precursor has been developed, in order to minimize the costly and damaging—to roadbeds and railroad beds—transportation of coal;

- Encourage each party to consider public-private partnerships to grow this industry;

- Ask executives of suppliers of aluminum and steel to auto, bus, and truck companies to diversify into carbon fiber manufacturing. Some of these suppliers are quite large companies, and may have the financial resources to build a carbon fiber manufacturing plant relatively quickly;

- Demand that such manufacturing plants operate in a way that inflict no harm on our environment. Require a thorough environmental impact statement by a neutral third party. It would be beyond irony to help launch an enterprise that slows climate change, only to find that its operation harms the environment in another way; for example, water pollution, soil erosion, toxic waste products. Vigilance will be required at each step of the way.

On the demand side, individuals can:

- Contact executives of U.S. automakers and urge an acceleration of the use of carbon fiber. If Lovins is correct, competition from German car manufacturers will certainly add urgency to this transition. For example, the BMW i3, rated at over 100 mpg, appears to lead in the use of carbon fiber for conventional cars, with its passenger compartment made of carbon fiber reinforced plastic (CFRP). A factory in the state of Washington makes CFRP for the BMW i3 and could presumably fabricate parts for other cars in their line, thereby reducing their weight and increasing their fuel efficiency and competitiveness. For years, Toyota could not keep up with the demand for the highly efficient Prius; I recall waiting about six months for my first one. Cars built with carbon fiber and offering fuel efficiency in excess of 100 mpg will repeat the pattern of demand outstripping supply for reason of economics, faith, the increasingly apparent dangers of climate change, or a combination of all three. As evidence, BMW reports that about 80 percent of i3 customers are purchasing a BMW for the first time, rather than being previous customers and, in addition, many are first-time car buyers.[2] This fuel efficient electric vehicle is clearly drawing people to this option. Aside from the environmental imperative, Americans might work to persuade U.S. car companies not to be caught again years behind in the use of a new technology.

- Become stockholders of the car companies and offer resolutions for consideration at annual meetings;
- Demonstrate at company headquarters calling for this transition;
- Conduct actions similar to the above at bus and truck companies;
- Contact executives of companies that manufacture small private and corporate aircraft to switch from steel and aluminum to carbon fiber; obvious benefits of the transition include improving the plane's fuel efficiency, increasing its range, and reducing the owner's operating costs.

All of the actions recommended in this chapter and the following on electricity generation comprise part of the environmental rights movement (ERM). That movement must be multifaceted, for we seek a huge drop in the combustion of coal, oil, and, eventually, natural gas. Individuals must drive this movement, people who form the "moral man," exerting power against reluctant, amoral (sometimes immoral) bureaucracies.

Thus, it is incumbent upon the environmental rights movement to remain mindful of one way Lovins has been effective: by demonstrating that proposed changes will accrue to the organization's financial benefit— but not by the next quarterly report. The environmental rights movement must accompany calls for change with figures making a reasonable business case for the shift, with that business case including reference to the environment in which that product will maintain its desirability.

---

2. *http://transportevolved.com/2014/06/09/bmw-i3-isnt-just-bmw-fans-premium-buyers-says-bmw-exec/*

18

Transforming Electricity Generation

Online petitions, Internet search engines, and social media have greatly increased the ability to obtain data on critical issues, organize protests for change, and solicit financial support. These mechanisms did not exist at the time of the civil rights movement and, as powerful as that was, the web and social media available now enable the possibility of an even more forceful environmental rights movement. Social media and web resources facilitate the transformative action sought by an environmental rights movement and, by themselves, almost answer the question, "What can I do?" A website can become the central point where information is gathered and other information disseminated about a particular environmental initiative.

These chapters offer specific ways for individuals to translate belief into action. One key point is participation: Many people contribute to environmental organizations and, as important and beneficial as that is, are not otherwise engaged with the organization.

I am urging something different: direct, personal actions. While it is true that the leadership of any effort does the bulk of the work, when members are asked to respond and participate, we must do so; sometimes it may not be possible, but "inconvenient" is not an excuse. When asked to send e-mails to corporate executives, we send them; and when asked to protest against a carbon-emitting operation, we show up and protest.

And 50,000 people responded to such a call for the Forward on Climate demonstration urging President Obama not to approve construction of the Keystone XL pipeline that would carry heavily polluting tar sands from Canada to the Gulf of Mexico. Organized by 350.org, The Sierra Club, and the Hip Hop Caucus, the gathering on February 17, 2013 constituted the largest pro-environment rally ever held—until the 400,000 strong People's Climate March in New York City in September 2014.

We are embarked on a historic transformation, ending the use of fossil fuels to power our society. Not by returning to a pre-industrial revolution world, but by moving forward to a non-polluting one. We wish to continue an America that can provide clean food, air, water, and energy for its population. We want the same for all the peoples of the world. Yet this movement is up against the "immoral society," as Niebuhr termed it: powerful, wealthy industries focused on short-term profit. But the "moral society" can prevail if we exert power against power, for our numbers are so great. That's why achieving the goal of a hospitable planet requires the active participation of large numbers of individuals. The "power" of the moral society is akin to that used by Dr. King: non-violent confrontations, marches, demonstrations, and speeches.

Coal-fired electricity generation plants constitute the largest stationary source of CO_2 emissions. Electricity generation accounted for 44 percent of all industrial toxic air pollution in 2010, exceeding those of the next two largest sectors combined (chemicals and paper products).[1]

Public advocacy, that is, personal, sustained involvement in helping to accomplish specific objectives, is needed to reduce CO_2 emissions. The initial objectives listed earlier include:

- Closing coal-fired electricity generation plants;
- Instituting a price on CO_2-producing energy sources;
- Constructing third generation nuclear plants; and,
- Promoting congregational and personal energy efficiency and the use of renewable energy.

A good deal of information about electricity generation plants is publicly available, which enables advocates to substantiate their calls for action with measured data. For example, each utility, as well as the Department of Energy (DOE), gathers detailed information about emissions from a plant's operations. Individuals can contact either the utility or DOE's Energy Information Administration and ask for figures on the CO_2 emissions from the utility's

---

1. "Toxic Power: How Power Plants Contaminate Our Air and States," National Resources Defense Council, August 2012, 8.

plants and the kilowatt hours (or millions of watt hours, megawatt hours) each plant produced. Then one can identify the plant with the highest emissions or, for the technically minded, the largest amount of CO_2 per unit of electricity produced (divide the pounds of CO_2 by megawatt hours of electricity). Once the worst plant has been determined, advocate for its closure or conversion to natural gas—that cuts CO_2 emissions by about half.[2]

Advocates can press for changes in electricity generation through:

- Widespread publicity of both the effort and the utility's response, including its intransigence, if that's the case;
- Persuading large shareholders of the utility's stock to sell their holdings, driving down the stock price (350.org began promoting this in 2012);
- Encouraging the utility's large customers to meet some of their electricity needs through their own fuel cells or renewable energy sources, thus eroding the utility's sales.

All such actions can be accompanied by a continuing number of speeches, marches, and demonstrations to show the community that the goal is to prevent another four million metric tons (or whatever the number) of CO_2 from entering the atmosphere.

Part of the work for advocates is to demonstrate that viable alternatives exist. We can't just propose reducing the existing capacity, but must demonstrate that more desirable approaches exist and that they make economic sense. Actions a utility could take to provide the needed capacity include:

- Conduct additional comprehensive programs to reduce the need (demand) for electricity from the commercial, industrial, and residential sectors;
- Convert the coal plant to a natural gas one, or purchase electricity from another entity that has generated it from renewable or nuclear energy;
- Install high capacity fuel cells at major electricity users under some type of lease or shared-purchase agreement;
- Explore providing the capacity by nuclear energy, biomass, or solar or wind energy; the total U.S. wind energy capacity is about 66,000 MW,

---

2. That 2:1 advantage may not hold up, however. Some researchers have suggested that drilling for gas by fracking can release a significant amount of methane into the atmosphere, and that gas has 21 times the global warming potential of carbon dioxide.

about half of China's installed capacity of 114,000 MW.[3] Texas, with 14,200 MW, leads the country, with California second (5,900 MW) and Iowa third (5,700 MW).[4] These impressive figures demonstrate that investors have found wind power economically attractive.[5]

Wind power, the energy source not visible except for its effects, resonates with descriptions both sacred and secular, with creation and topography. The opening of Genesis gives us:

> In the beginning when God created the heavens and the earth, the earth was a formless void and darkness covered the face of the deep, while a wind from God swept over the face of the waters. . . .

Gen. 1:1–2

Wind blew before God said "Let there be light." Wind is our primeval energy source. A secular and a contemporary reference given by David Foster Wallace described how that force shaped life in his hometown.:

> But mostly wind. The biggest single factor in Central Illinois' quality of outdoor life is wind. There are more local jokes than I can summon about bent weather vanes and leaning barns, more downstate sobriquets for kinds of wind than there are in Malamut for snow. The wind had a personality, a (poor) temper, and, apparently, agendas.[6]

How satisfying, then, to generate electricity though wind power. While huge blades mounted about 200 feet into the air provide our primary image of wind energy, several new designs, of varying capacities, offer alternatives that may be more efficient, less costly, and not result in bird kills. The Saphon company, of Tunisia, has a bladeless wind turbine that purports to deliver greater efficiency at lower cost.[7] A New York firm has designed

---

3. *http://www.gwec.net/global-figures/graphs/*

4. *http://apps2.eere.energy.gov/wind/windexchange/wind_installed_capacity.asp*

5. Attractive, to some degree, because of the subsidies that had been in place. But the subsidies existed to encourage doing something different, to encourage the transition from fossil fuels to renewables. If one agrees that the buildup of CO_2 in the atmosphere is changing our climate, then subsidies to accelerate a transition make sense.

6. From *A Supposedly Fun Thing I'll Never Do Again* by David Foster Wallace, Copyright © 1997 by David Foster Wallace, 4. Used by permission of Little, Brown and Company.

7. *http://www.treehugger.com/wind-technology/new-bladeless-wind-turbine-claimed-be-twice-efficient-conventional-designs.html*

Windstalks that, indeed, look like tall stalks blowing in the wind and through their movement generate electricity.[8] Solar Aero, a New Hampshire-based company, has developed the Fuller wind turbine, which has no exposed blades, for small applications.[9] Thus wind turbines of increasing efficiency and without bird kills definitely appear feasible—and we can advocate for them by pressing our utility and Public Utility Commission to consider wind power to meet some electricity needs.

The familiar term "supply and demand" can be applied to carbon emissions associated with electricity generation. The section above described actions to reduce the amount of electricity generated at coal-fired power plants. That's the supply side: how electricity is supplied to us. The other part is the demand side: how Americans can reduce the need, or demand, for electricity *from the grid*. Recall that the grid is the term used to describe the complex of transmission and distribution power lines that move electricity from generating stations to homes, offices, and factories. Until grid-supplied electricity is provided mainly by non-polluting energy rather than from fossil fuels, reducing demand from the grid is of paramount importance.

To lower demand, homeowners and building owners can install photovoltaic (PV) panels to generate electricity for their facilities. Every hour that electricity comes from these panels means an hour during which we, individually, are not causing carbon to enter the atmosphere and thereby worsen the climate change problem.[10] Home and office buildings would remain connected to the grid, but while the sun is shining some of the building's electricity would be supplied by a non-polluting source. During the night, the electricity need generally goes down and that electricity can come from the grid. In future years, some of that nighttime electricity could come from a wind farm or a battery pack such as the Powerwall from Tesla Energy, mentioned earlier, and the need for fossil-fuel-supplied electricity would diminish further.[11]

---

8. *http://news.discovery.com/tech/alternative-power-sources/windpower-without-blades-101015.htm*

9. *http://phys.org/news192426996.html*

10. This follows because as a homeowner uses electricity from an on-site PV array, less electricity is required from the grid; thus, the utility senses a reduced demand. This is different from a large PV installation serving as a generating station for renewable energy; the utility cannot yet count on this, for its output varies with cloud cover and time of day.

11. As mentioned earlier, the grid must provide a stable source of electricity. Wind- and solar-provided energy can drop in minutes. Research and development are needed to integrate renewable energy onto the grid with sufficient reserve storage and weather predictability so that conventional synchronous generators can compensate for predicted fluctuations from renewable sources.

Installing PV panels on a home or office building is an individual or corporate decision, not dependent on permission from a slow-moving government bureaucracy. We can make the decision for reasons of finances and faith, in any combination, without seeking permission from an entity without a personal stake in our enterprise. Thus, we can make the decision quickly. We do need the cooperation of the utility company, however, and must ensure the utility does not slow down or block an installation.

Lovins references a 2008 paper[12] stating that one-third of total U.S. electricity demand could be met by installing solar PV on well-suited roof space. What a profound effect that would have: reducing carbon emissions from conventional generation by about a third when solar energy is available, either from the sun or from a battery pack, if that technology proves reliable.

With sustained federal and state tax credits, many homeowners and building owners could be persuaded to do this. Evidence for this comes from a report that installations of residential photovoltaic systems reached 232 MW in the first quarter of 2014, roughly double what was installed in the first quarter of 2012—that's a remarkable growth rate.[13] In addition to whatever financial argument could be made—a function of panel cost, installation, and tax credits—users benefit by reducing their vulnerability to grid electricity outages[14] and exposure to volatile energy prices, and can rightfully highlight their contribution to slowing climate change. The total installed PV capacity through the first quarters of 2015 is estimated at 16.1 GW, with another 1.4 GW in concentrating solar power capacity.

Installing PV panels to supply part of the electricity and reduce the carbon emissions that currently result from fossil-fuel-supplied power constitutes one recommended personal action for homeowners and building owners.

---

12. Lovins, *Reinventing Fire*, 205, reference 631.

13. *http://www.seia.org/news/us-residential-solar-pv-installations-*

14. If users have a battery-backup system.

19

Close to Home

Carbon emissions decrease as product efficiencies increase. If we each can recall that simple fact and act on it, we will slow down climate change. As each person makes product energy efficiency a top priority with any purchase, the amount of carbon released into the atmosphere decreases.

If we think our one purchase does not make a difference, we might consider the following two ideas:

- People in Kansas, California, Iowa, New York, and elsewhere are making similar decisions; we are a country of about 350 million people. We want individuals in other states to make the environmentally appropriate decision, and they want us to do the same. Both wishes will only come true if we all feel the same obligation—to support our fellow Americans, our neighbors: "You shall love your neighbor as yourself."
- "I do not need to behave morally this time, because most of the time I do. This is just a minor transgression." We know such reasoning is nonsense. If we are given the gift of such awareness, then a response might be a silent "thank you" for the reminder. Many people share the belief that we are ultimately answerable for our choices—each of them, whether large or small.

Thus, the two ideas that slowing climate change requires a *collective effort* formed of countless *individual spiritual/moral decisions* should act as retaining walls that keep us headed toward environmental improvement.

As we purchase energy-using equipment for our homes, businesses, and congregations, information about energy efficiency is available in numerous books and websites, some of which are listed at the end of this chapter. The Environmental Protection Agency (EPA) and the Department of Energy (DOE) offer a variety of particularly helpful resources.

One EPA web page,[1] for example, lists all ENERGY STAR qualified equipment[2] and has calculators that determine the annual and life cycle costs for operating a product and the amount of CO_2 emitted each year. A user can enter the costs for the ENERGY STAR and conventional products and the local electricity rate, and determine what each would cost annually and over its lifetime. This website includes information about ENERGY STAR qualified food service equipment as well, which can be quite energy intensive. Another site,[3] hosted by the Food Service Technology Center, covers a broader range of products and topics that apply to this sector.

A companion site[4] hosted by the DOE contains similar information about both non–ENERGY STAR and ENERGY STAR products, and the two sites give buyers access to a wealth of efficiency information about a wide range of products.

Home and business computers should be turned off at night, and business systems should also be off on weekends, unless people are working. Computers in offices are sometimes left on to enable a company server to transmit a software update at night. This can be a costly protocol. Another EPA website[5] identifies software that can place a network of computers into sleep mode after business hours, and only "wake" the computers when the server is about to transmit the update.

The EPA also offers a web-based, no cost, computational tool called Portfolio Manager (PM) that determines the energy efficiency of a building relative to a large population of similar buildings across the country. A congregation could use this to evaluate the efficiency of its space. Portfolio Manager uses a 1–100 scale to denote efficiency, and one feature in the software enables the user to determine the reduction in energy use and cost if efficiency upgrades were made that raised the building's score some number of points. The lower the rating the more one is paying for energy, and the less the institution has available to fund its core activities. Portfolio Manager handles a wide range of building types, including office buildings, K–12 schools, houses of worship, and senior care facilities.

---

1. *www.energystar.gov/products/certified-products?s=footer*

2. This equipment is more energy efficient than conventional equipment, having met specifications for superior energy performance agreed to by the EPA and product manufacturers. ENERGY STAR is a multifaceted program of the EPA.

3. *www.fishnick.com*

4. *http://energy.gov/eere/femp/energy-and-cost-savings-calculators-energy-efficient-products*

5. *www.energystar.gov/powermanagement*

Another EPA site[6] provides a similar rating tool, but this one for buildings being designed. The online software, called Target Finder, enables building owners, architects, and engineers to determine a planned building's annual energy use corresponding to a user-specified level of energy performance (1–100 scale). For example, if a building owner wants the performance of a new facility to be among the top 10 percent in the country, a designer can quickly determine what that corresponds to in energy per square foot per year. In addition, Target Finder provides a design team with the building's rating corresponding to its estimated energy use (for example, kWh per year, therms of natural gas per year). These two computational tools can contribute to one of Lovins's key objectives: reducing energy use in buildings.

Understanding the difference between site and source energy can help one decide between an electric or gas-powered product. Natural gas, coal, and oil used for heating are usually consumed at a building's site, with the heat energy converted into mechanical energy to do work. Electrical energy, however, results from several energy conversion processes that take place at an electricity generating station, one powered by coal, natural gas, or nuclear energy. The electricity is transmitted to a site over power lines. The energy expended at a generating plant is far more than what reaches the site, for losses occur in the generation, transmission, and distribution of electricity.

The EPA estimates that about three times more CO_2 is emitted into the atmosphere per million Btu[7] of energy from electricity than per million Btu from natural gas. Thus, energy provided by natural gas results in fewer emissions than the equivalent amount of energy provided by electricity. This can factor into one's decision about purchasing an electric or gas clothes dryer or water heater, for example.

Using electricity generated by an on-site solar array (photovoltaic panels, PV) results in no carbon emissions, and consequently represents a superior choice for congregations, homes, and businesses. PV panels provide the additional benefit of operating despite a local or widespread power outage, if they have battery backup. A variety of state tax credits[8] and utility

---

6. *www.energystar.gov/commercialbuildingdesign*

7. Btu, or British thermal unit: the amount of heat needed to raise the temperature of one pound of water by one degree Fahrenheit.

8. The website *www.dsireusa.org* can be quite helpful with this.

incentive programs, in addition to federal tax credits, can make this a financially, as well as environmentally, attractive option. Additional resources to improve home energy efficiency include the following:

Books

The Homeowner's Energy Handbook by Paul Scheckel (North Adams, MA: Story Publishing, 2013).

Go Green, Save Green: A Simple Guide to Saving Time, Money and God's Green Earth by Nancy Sleeth (Carol Stream, IL: Tyndale Press, 2009).

Black & Decker, The Complete Guide to a Green Home by Philip Schmidt (Minneapolis: Creative Publishing International, 2008).

Insulate & Weatherize by Bruce Harley (Newtown, CT: Taunton Press, 2012).

Renovations, 4th Edition, by Michael W. Litchfield (Newtown, CT: Taunton Press, 2012).

The Solar House: Passive solar heating and cooling by Daniel D. Chiras (White River Junction, VT: Chelsea Green Publishing Company, , 2002).

Websites

http://energy.gov/energysaver/downloads/energy-savers-guide/

http://www.energystar.gov/index.cfm?c=home_improvement.hm_improvement_index

http://energy.gov/public-services/homes

https://www.progress-energy.com/carolinas/home/save-energy-money/energy-saving-tips-calculators/100-tips.page

http://homeenergysaver.lbl.gov/consumer/

http://energy.gov/eere/femp/home-energy-checklist

http://www.aceee.org/consumer

20

The Matter of Faith

Twenty-three years after the historic Rio conference on climate change in 1992, efforts are underway in the U.S. to reduce the effects of climate change in the four areas identified by Lovins: electricity generation, buildings, transportation, and industry. The buildings, transportation, and industrial sectors have reduced emissions, some faster and more steeply than others, and the administration of President Obama took major steps with electricity generation.

During President Obama's first term, the administration made loans to accelerate the research and development of renewable energy technologies. In his second term, the administration proposed rules for existing and new coal-fired power plants that, once implemented, will reduce CO_2 emissions about 30 percent from 2005 levels. This constitutes a substantive move by the executive branch, one deserving of thanks by all wishing to preserve a hospitable planet.

My personal belief is that the second term announcement of new rules merited a presidential address on climate change to clarify the reasons for and urgency of such regulations and build public support. Sadly, that did not happen, as it also did not occur in the first term with renewable energy loans.[1] National transformations call for national announcements.

---

1. As one consequence, President Obama's Republican challenger in 2012 was able to escape the consequences of falsely stating the success rate of research and development loans as only 50 percent and almost mocking this expenditure of public money. In fact, only 3 of 33 companies that received loans have failed, yielding a success rate of about 91 percent and a loss of less than 2 percent of the money budgeted. (the *New York Times*, The Editorial Page Editor's Blog, "About that $90 Billion Green Energy Tax Break," Robert B. Semple Jr., October 4, 2012.) The loans represented an example of leadership so desperately needed. With one of the highest per capita rates of CO_2 emissions among developed nations and total emissions second only to China (three times our population), what the U.S. does and advocates has enormous influence on the fate of the world's climate.

Nevertheless, we are fortunate that efforts toward a national transformation away from fossil fuels are also underway with environmental organizations such as 350.org, National Resources Defense Council (NRDC), Environmental Defense Fund (EDF), and the Sierra Club pushing for change, and by individuals whose purchasing decisions are heavily influenced by product energy efficiency.

The fact that within the span of one lifetime the climate in North America and elsewhere will change significantly requires difficult-to-comprehend shifts in our way of life. The rainfall, storms, and seasonal temperatures to which we, our parents, and grandparents became accustomed[2] will change, affecting the availability and cost of food and water, the clothes we wear, energy expenses, travel, and significantly altering our vulnerability to a variety of threats. Climate change that occurs over millennia poses little difficulty in absorbing, but a compression of the timeframe to half a century is altogether new and understandably scary. Climate change is one of the most important issues humans have faced since our prehistoric ancestor Lucy walked the terrain of Africa.

The U.S. is doing many of the right things to deal with climate change, but at a pace that will doom us to suffer devastating and irreversible consequences.

Our slow pace of response is incompatible with the fast pace of carbon buildup. From the start of the industrial revolution in the eighteenth century to about 1970, atmospheric CO_2 was increasing at a rate of about 0.25 ppm per year. That rate is now almost 10 times faster, or about 2.0 ppm per year. That alarming change offers compelling evidence that the CO_2 increase arises not from "natural" processes, but from how we now live upon this planet—specifically, our heavy use of fossil fuels for energy. (See Figure 6, chapter 12.)

In the context of actions to slow climate change, our rate of change in remedial measures is inadequate to the problem at hand. It is vitally important that we move quickly on the first nine of the ten items discussed in chapter 16.

What is the desirable rate of reduction of CO_2 emissions? Selecting Lovins's goal of an 80 percent reduction in emissions by 2050 would serve as a reasonable starting point.

---

2. As well as for the birds of the sky, the fish of the sea, and everything that moves on the land—and all plant life as well.

Why isn't the pace faster in the U.S.? Why aren't more individuals, companies, and utilities making the changes listed above? Because many powerful forces, the "immoral society" to use Niebuhr's term, work to slow them down. For example:

- Energy companies that use their vast wealth to lobby Congress and state legislatures to continue a business-as-usual policy, and use the media to deny or question the validity of climate change findings;
- Government officials who, either out of ignorance or self-interest, use their position to oppose legislation that would reduce carbon emissions, or espouse policies that would increase them;
- Corporate executives who withhold energy-efficiency investments because of their potential impact on the next quarterly report. Does it make sense for a forty-year-old company to have a time horizon of three months?

One industry that does accept the reality of climate change is the insurance industry. A *Scientific American*[3] article reports that, "Weather-related insurance losses rose to $50 billion in 2005 from less than $10 billion a decade earlier . . ." A June 2013 report from the Geneva Association[4] states that "There is new, robust evidence that the global oceans have warmed significantly. Given that energy from the ocean is the key driver of extreme events, ocean warming has effectively caused a shift towards a 'new normal' for a number of insurance relevant hazards," and continues that ". . . even if greenhouse gas (GHG) emissions completely stop tomorrow, oceanic temperatures will continue to rise." Later in the Summary they write that, "In some high-risk areas, ocean warming and climate change threaten the insurability of catastrophe risk more generally."

We face the question, therefore, of how to deal with powerful institutions that impede actions on climate change. Efforts that persist despite extreme weather events such as tornados, floods, fires, and droughts, as well as Hurricane Katrina of 2005 and Superstorm Sandy of 2012—and extremes of weather constitute only one result, though a highly visible one,

---

3. Victoria Schlesinger and Meredith Knight, "Insurers Claim Global Warming Makes Some Regions Too Hot to Handle," *Scientific American*, August 1, 2007.

4. "Warming of the Oceans and Implications for the (Re)insurance Industry," The Geneva Association, 2012, 3. Used with permission. The Association identifies itself as "the leading international insurance think tank for strategically important insurance and risk management issues."

of climate change. For example, routinely visible, palpable, and unhealthful air pollution persists in China and India's major cities, both caused mainly by emissions from coal-fired power plants and cars.[5]

The three opposing forces listed represent major sectors of our society: the government, the energy industry, and some large corporations. How do we overcome such formidable opposition? By launching an effort, described in Part II, analogous to how Martin Luther King Jr. led the civil rights movement: In sermons and speeches the Rev. Dr. King argued that maintaining racial segregation was not only damaging to our society, but was morally wrong. That moral aspect immediately raised the discussion to a level that connected with deeply held religious beliefs of many people and to which institutions had difficulty responding.[6] Similarly, our heavy use of fossil fuels for energy is not only damaging our planet, but is morally wrong. This book and others have demonstrated that, but I fear such evidence will remain insufficiently motivating until proclaimed by a representative of the faith community who is part of the leadership of the environmental movement. With arguments for action based on matters of faith, alongside science and economics, opposing institutions are disadvantaged: An energy company may dispute the findings of climate science—it cannot rebut a teaching of Jesus or a verse in Deuteronomy.

Our faith-based argument to slow climate change by reducing carbon emissions came from a principle deduced from teachings in the "Law" and the commentary called the Talmud: individuals are not to engage in activities that injure the community. This principle is rooted in familiar verses such as:

In everything do to others as you would have them do to you . . .

from Matt. 7:12

". . . but you shall love your neighbor as yourself"

from Lev. 19:18

You shall love your neighbor as yourself.

from Matt. 22:39 and Mark 12:31

---

5. *http://www.theguardian.com/environment/2013/jul/08/northern-china-air-pollution-life-expectancy*

6. As mentioned earlier, some congregations were very slow to respond, as the Rev. King explicitly noted in the letter written from a Birmingham jail.

We must read these guiding principles with a new mindset.

We have lived with the idea that our neighbor is someone close enough to be directly affected by our actions. We now know that our neighbor can be on the other side of the world, for our actions, particularly the carbon we send into the atmosphere, directly affects them. That's the new reality!

Christians cannot simultaneously express love for the Father and the Son and be content with inflicting pain on others, their neighbors, and on God's creation. Jews face the same quandary, for those principles are part of Hebrew Scripture. In addition, we have these words that Midrash[7] teaches God spoke to Adam in the Garden:

> See my works, how fine and excellent they are! Now all that I have created, for you have I created. Think upon this and do not corrupt and desolate My World, For if you corrupt it, there is no one to set it right after you.

This ancient cautionary note takes contemporary form in a teaching of Pope Francis: "Safeguard Creation. Because if we destroy Creation, Creation will destroy us. Never forget this!"[8]

Earlier in that message, the pope explained:

> Creation is not a property, which we can rule over at will; or, even less, is the property of only a few: Creation is a gift, it is a wonderful gift that God has given us, so that we care for it and we use it for the benefit of all, always with great respect and gratitude.

Pope Francis then pinpoints a transgression of our times:

> But when we exploit Creation we destroy the sign of God's love for us, in destroying Creation we are saying to God: "I don't like it! This is not good!" "So what do you like?" "I like myself!"—Here, this is sin!

People for whom the Hebrew and Christian scriptures are sacred must bring together the multiple efforts underway to slow climate change,

---

7. A Midrash is a story that expands or clarifies a biblical teaching. This one is from Ecclesiastes Rabbah 7:28.

8. From a lesson delivered by Pope Francis on May 21, 2014. *www.news.va/en/news/pope-at-audience-if-we-destroy-creation-it-will-de*. ©Libreria Editrice Vaticana and © Radio Vaticana for English Translation. Used with permission

and supplement them, to launch an environmental rights movement that appeals to the three-part argument of faith, science, and economics.

The civil rights movement led by Dr. King included close advisors, likely co-leaders, from secular groups such as attorneys and community organizers. The leadership of the environmental rights movement must similarly include pastors and persons of deep faith in order to ensure the call for change emanates from that tripartite argument.

The civil rights movement was launched and led by Martin Luther King Jr., and other African-American pastors and, in this sense, was initially a faith-based movement seeking racial equality. The movement was joined by thousands of people, eventually millions, whose support for the cause was not primarily faith-based, yet reflected a firm belief in its objectives.

In contrast, efforts to slow climate change and preserve our environment were launched and continue to be driven primarily by numerous organizations drawings on arguments of science, economics, and the law, with collectively millions of people supporting their objectives. These efforts must be joined by large groups of individuals from diverse denominations whose commitment to their faith motivates them to preserve God's creation. Many such groups already exist, but their numbers must swell. Seeing a pastor or person of deep faith in the leadership of the movement will understandably serve as a magnet for others. These two large coalitions must then coalesce into an environmental rights movement,

We have the right to an environment that supports life

in which the existing environmental organizations, both secular and religious, continue to operate, but allocate much of their resources to furthering the united environmental rights movement co-directed by a secular-based and faith-based leadership.

The religious leadership of the environmental rights movement must emerge from the actions of people of faith. That is, the leadership should come from whichever groups take up this cause with the greatest energy. There are literally dozens of meaningful game-changing actions individuals and community groups can undertake, and the leadership should emerge from those groups that demonstrate the wisdom and effectiveness of their actions.

One of the effective tools at our disposal is online petitions, and we have seen that they can bring swift and meaningful change. A fourth-grade class in Brookline, Massachusetts wrote a petition asking Universal Studios to modify the website about an upcoming movie based on the story *The Lorax*, by Dr. Seuss. The students were angry that the website seemed to ignore the core message of the book: to take care of nature, to protect the trees. The petition quickly gathered over fifty thousand signatures, and the studio modified the website to include the environmental message for which the students petitioned.

Two other online petitions persuaded Verizon and Bank of America to cancel newly proposed fees. Those two huge corporations responded within days to the tens of thousands of customers who expressed outrage and demanded change.

The Internet and social media put tremendous power into the hands of individuals, and they are tools the environmental rights movement must employ judiciously, though regularly, to preserve our planet. We can succeed if our actions are rooted in faith as well as science.

Secular arguments alone for rational behavior, for example, not destroying our own food supply and drinking water, will have a difficult time prevailing in our highly capitalistic society whose primary measure is money. But arguments rooted in our faith, our belief in God and God's teachings, transcend that capitalistic viewpoint.[9] A faith-led environmental rights movement can be as persuasive about preserving the natural world as the civil rights movement was about racial equality, that is, equality with jobs, housing, and voting. The current analog of those goals are the measures listed in chapter 16 that provide a path from coal and oil to renewables and nuclear energy. We can, of course, modify and adapt these measures as we proceed, but the time has come to make our actions reflect our faith. We need a new Dr. King to remind us of the undeniable connections between that path and our faith.

---

9. This is part of the message of Pope Francis in his Encyclical Letter *Laudato Si'*.

21

Choose Life

The list of climate change effects that have commanded our attention over recent years is dominated by painful episodic events such as tornados, fires, and floods. Our attention turns to other matters after the worst of each has passed, except for those in the affected areas who continue to mourn their dead, or look out on charred forests, or deal with the aftermath of flooded homes.

Climate change will soon inflict continual, not episodic, pain upon us. Bill McKibben, in his book *Eaarth*,[1] describes some of what the continuing effects of climate change will bring:

- The appearance of dengue fever, for which no vaccine and no real cure exists; if you're young, well fed, and in good health, the chances of surviving are pretty good; if any of those three are not the case, survival is less likely. The increase in cases of the tropical disease dengue fever is occurring because the Tropical Zone has been expanding at a rate of about 0.7 degrees per decade since the 1970s.[2]

- An increasing number of cases of West Nile virus: This serious disease not only affects our health, but also the economy because of the money needed to treat it and the productivity lost by those who contract it.

- A climate refugee population of as many as 700 million by mid-century, arising from loss of water supply, the incursion of salt water into fresh water regions, loss of arable land due to dust storms and oppressive heat, and other effects.

---

1. Bill McKibben, *Eaarth: Making a Life on a Tough New Planet* (New York: St. Martin's Griffen, 2011).

2. See *http://e360.yale.edu/digest/black_carbon_ozone_may_be_expanding_tropical_belt/3469/*

- A planet with multiple wars raging due to scarce resources. McKibben quotes from an article in *Fortune*[3] addressing the effects of climate change, and referencing one Department of Defense study forecasting potential scenarios only a decade or two away when the effects of climate change have become irrefutable. Consider potential conflicts among India, Pakistan, and China over refugees or the use of shared rivers, or between Spain and Portugal over fishing rights arising from fish migration because of warmer waters. As climate change hits home, manifesting in a diminished food supply, to cite one example, warfare may become a common element of human life.

- Lower Manhattan, south Florida, and hundreds of miles of U.S. coastline under frequent threat of flooding, requiring highly costly relocations of populations, businesses, and infrastructure. Superstorm Sandy of 2012 inflicted a devastating illustration of this on New Jersey and New York.

- Oppressively high summer temperatures in numerous cities, over-whelming electricity generation plants and leading to large numbers of heat-related deaths and lost business productivity.

- An increasing number of extreme events such as tornados, fires, floods, and hurricanes.

Unfortunately this list could expand to manuscript length, and McKibben's book is an excellent source for those seeking a more comprehensive picture. These climate change effects and numerous others will grow in both intensity and number as atmospheric CO_2 continues to rise.

But we have a choice, with our option expressed in biblical language in Deuteronomy 30:19–20: "Choose life so that you and your descendants may live, loving the LORD your God, obeying him, and holding fast to him." Colloquially, choose life over disease. Choose life over capricious storms. Choose life over hunger. Heed the teachings Part I has touched upon, and use the intelligence God gave us. Demand that we commit, understanding the urgency, to a transformation from fossil fuels to forms of energy that result in no greenhouse gas emissions.

This issue is a political one as well, for when we vote, we choose. Many of us have decades of loyalty to one political party, and sometimes that

---

3. David Stipp, "The Pentagon's Weather Nightmare. The climate could change radically, and fast. That would be the mother of all national security issues," *Fortune*, February. 9, 2004, 100–108.

loyalty has more influence on our vote than a candidate's positions on the issues. This must change!

If the welfare of your children, grandchildren, all children is important to you, then of necessity the future habitability of the planet is important to you. These are now inseparable.

Therefore, vote your self-interest and, if this is personally relevant, in accord with the teachings of your faith. Vote for candidates that agree that climate change is real and that human activities are the primary cause, and who commit to addressing the problem with the urgency required. Cast your vote based on a candidate's response to the issues, not because of party label. That may be difficult, but if we retain a concern for the wellbeing and happiness of our progeny, the choice of candidates will be made easier. Voting to mitigate climate change will not bring you discomfort. It will, however, improve the world for our children, our descendants. That's a good deal, and one that will bring about another transformation: the elevation of issues over party labels. Through this change, Americans can reduce the corrosive influence of money in politics, for it is we, we the people, who ultimately cast the ballots. It is we who choose.

22

Promote the General Welfare

This title comes from the preamble to the Constitution of the United States and identifies one of the core objectives of the document and the government regulated by it: to promote the general welfare. The welfare of people all across the U.S. has not, however, been promoted in the past decade, but rather battered by:

- Tornados that tore through parts of Missouri, Alabama, Arkansas, Tennessee, Georgia, Oklahoma, Mississippi, North Carolina, Virginia, and Iowa;
- Fires that torched parts of Texas, Colorado, Washington, Arizona, and California;
- Hurricanes that slammed coastal areas of Louisiana, Mississippi, North Carolina, South Carolina, and Florida;
- Superstorm Sandy, whose storm surges, winds, and rain devastated entire communities and the infrastructure of lower Manhattan; and,
- Floods that swamped parts of Missouri, Arkansas, Illinois, Mississippi, Tennessee, and Louisiana.

We know that the government dispatches the Federal Emergency Management Agency (FEMA) quickly, and the agency generally does a good job, with Hurricane Katrina a notable exception, of helping those whose lives have been shattered. Congress eventually allocates funds—$60 billion for Sandy—that go toward repairing and restoring the lost or damaged physical structures. The money cannot do much, however, to heal the trauma and emotional wounds victims have suffered, some of whom have a limited ability to cope and consequently may never recover.

The allocation of major funding from the federal government only begins the process of restoration and, in the case of Sandy at least, the money is not adequate to cover all repair work needed and the temporary housing of people who must leave damaged homes during the rebuilding. As the *New York Times* reported, twenty months after Sandy hundreds of families in the New York City area have been unable to complete repairs and remain in damaged dwellings.[1] Many residents continue to seek help from a slew of charitable organizations whose sheer number for one locality reflects the frustrating task of helping people return to habitable buildings: the New York City Unmet Needs Roundtable; Build It Back; Brooklyn Long-Term Recovery Group; Resurrection Brooklyn; Arab-American Family Support Center; and Gerritsen Beach Cares. More and more Americans will find themselves in a similar state of limbo as climate-change-induced storms and floods pummel us, and bureaucracies remain unable to respond in an adequate and timely manner.

Government must promote the general welfare by taking steps to protect our population before disaster strikes, to prevent emotionally crippling losses: the disintegration of the bedroom in which our children slept, the drenching of family photos, the drowning of a handicapped friend by an early storm surge. Disasters will strike with increasing fury and frequency in future years, and leave in their wake an increasing number of wounded souls and governments at all levels deeper in debt. A few examples of preventive measures include:

- Enhance tornado early warning systems and ways to reach people;
- Acquire more firefighting equipment and hire staff to operate it;
- Discourage development of any kind in coastal areas known to be at risk;
- Construct barricades to protect against storm surges.

The last item sounds like a big one, given the size of the U.S. coastline, but we know the locations that are particularly vulnerable and we have the engineering know-how to construct such protection. It seems far more reasonable to spend $60 billion on protection than to spend $600 billion repairing the damage caused by ten storms. Superstorm Sandy, though

---

1. Liz Robbins, "After the Storm, 20 Months in Limbo," *New York Times*, June 22, 2014, 26–27.

unusual in its size and ferocity, was not the last painful and costly storm Americans will endure; for example, the powerful nor'easter storm of January 2015 brought declarations of snow emergencies in six states and travel bans in four.

Great Britain built a barricade in the Thames River to prevent London from flooding. Completed around 1982, it has been used more than a hundred times.[2]

The Netherlands continues to build large barricades to protect its inherently vulnerable land and people; the country has a hundred-year plan to deal with climate change.[3] About 26 percent of the country lies below sea level and roughly 60 percent of the population lives on that portion.

In 2015, our government does not yet have a plan, though individual city, county, and state governments have developed about a hundred adaptation plans. However, with the exception of New York City's $19.5 billion plan, most others lack specificity.[4] The intensity of recent weather events and the devastation they have caused call for action: For each particularly vulnerable locale, the federal government can help to customize realistic plans and suggest public-private partnerships to bring them to fruition.

Those who believe such protective measures are unnecessary, for they deny the science of climate change or reject the finding that human actions are the primary cause, place themselves in a very awkward position. These same people likely consult newspapers, the Internet, or phones for weather predictions, and assume they are reasonably accurate; accept the science of medicine when they visit doctors and take drugs; accept the science of flight when they board airplanes; accept the science of communication when they access the web, send e-mails, and answer phone calls. Only the science of climate change is suspect.

We know scientific findings do not carry 100 percent accuracy. However, given the evidence on hand and the excellent correlation between theory and measurement discussed earlier (see Figure 6 in chapter 12), denials appear based on greed or personal wishes, not on an alternative analysis of

---

2. *www.environment-agency.gov.uk/homeandleisure/floods/117047.aspx*

3. *http://blogs.worldwatch.org/sustainableprosperity/leading-by-example-the-dutch-prepare-for-climate-change/*

4. *http://insideclimatenews.org/news/20130620/6-worlds-most-extensive-climate-adaptation-plans*

the voluminous data. In fact, most denials constitute a "shadow play," to use Herbert Needleman's expression—arguments without substance meant to prolong business as usual.

Public officials who deny a correlation between the use of fossil fuels and climate change are failing their constitutional obligation to "promote the general welfare." People who use their positions of power to obstruct the phasing out of coal and oil, and to block the transition to renewable energy, are not only failing their responsibility and betraying their country but, from one perspective, are behaving immorally.

Similarly, Martin Luther King Jr. expressed disappointment in his letter written from a Birmingham jail in 1963, eight years after the Montgomery bus boycott, about the church (pastors and rabbis of the "white church") still remaining largely uninvolved in the struggle for integration, of not seeing the cause as "morally right." Then, with the passage of the Civil Rights Act of 1964 and the Voting Rights Act of 1965, integration began to take hold and its legal and moral correctness were gradually embraced by the country and the church.

But as many parishioners remembered that the church was largely absent from advocating for this morally correct cause, the moral authority of the church began to weaken, I believe.

We the people, and the church, now confront another secular issue, climate change, with once again a deep moral component: devastating God's creation and causing increasing pain for "the least of these."

Once again, with notable exceptions, the church has not been part of the leadership of this movement, though that is beginning to change: the leaders of several Protestant denominations and the leader of the Roman Catholic Church have issued clear statements about care of God's creation—mitigating climate change—as a religious/spiritual issue.[5] It is as if they are responding to the warning of the Rev. Fletcher Harper, quoted earlier, "If religion cannot provide meaningful leadership on one of the most pressing issues facing the human family, then it will lose its ability to present itself as a moral force."[6] I believe that an unrelenting

---

5. Denominations and movements within Judaism have also released strong statements about climate change as a religious, as well as an environmental, issue. The groups include: the Union of Reform Judaism; the Rabbinical Assembly of Conservative Judaism; the Jewish Renewal movement; the Jewish Reconstructionist Federation; and the Orthodox Union.

6. "I Believe Three Things," 165.

message from the church, accompanied by sustained pressure from congregants, non-congregants, and shareholders, will move business leaders and lawmakers at all levels to begin rejecting specious denials of human responsibility for the damage experienced and that predicted. Business and government leaders will tacitly admit that long-term (more than one quarter into the future) economic self-interest requires them to act in preservation of the environment in which they have flourished for so long.

People of faith understand that religion is *lived*, not just observed. Many decisions we make have a moral component. People persuaded either by the preponderance of scientific evidence or the morality of a speedy transition away from fossil fuels must join together to keep our planet hospitable to life.

And in the U.S., it does require the people—*We, the people*—to bring about the changes. It does fall to governments to regulate our infrastructure and to install protective barriers, but it is inherently our job to force a departure from business as usual. Our government can seem a slow-moving bureaucracy, often incapacitated by competing political agendas, and therefore unable to act with the urgency required. Some of this is built-in, for in our representative democracy governments rarely get ahead of the people—that is, truly lead. When the will of the people is unmistakable, though, governments respond. That's what occurred with the civil rights movement, and I believe we will see the pattern repeated.

Fortunately, as Lovins wrote, the transformation from fossil fuels to non-polluting energy does not require an Act of Congress, but cost-effective changes throughout our commercial, industrial and, ultimately, residential sectors. We the people can push, prod, demonstrate, and insist on this in numerous ways. If the weapon of online petitions can gain tens of thousands of supporters within hours and cause major corporations to reverse policies, we realize that an entire arsenal of tools awaits our use to accomplish the energy transformation required.

We the people will bring about the tipping point that will launch America into wide-scale use of radiation from the sun, the force of the wind, and the power of the atom to deliver the energy for our needs. And, we know that a failure to act is a spiritual/religious failure: It is immoral to willfully cause injury to all life on earth and condemn future generations to a struggle for survival on a planet that once lovingly provided for the sustenance of all of God's creatures.

Our descendants would never forgive our choosing expediency over preserving a hospitable planet. When people driven more by faith than science join forces with those driven more by science than faith, their union will form the Environmental Rights Movement that will stabilize the earth's climate and preserve God's creation.

ABOUT EDUCATION FOR MINISTRY

Do you have questions about your faith? Most people do, and most find it challenging to get answers. Education for Ministry (EfM) was developed by the School of Theology in Sewanee, Tennessee, to provide a mechanism for people to work through those questions. This four-year course of study is led by a mentor who provides the framework for the group to connect faith to their daily lives through reading and discussion.

Meeting once a week in small groups with people from your neighborhood, you will begin to think theologically, reflect faithfully, and speak civilly when confronted by beliefs and principles in opposition to your own. And that's something we can all appreciate in today's world.

By being an EfM participant, you will learn how to articulate your faith. You will learn how to shape your faith into action. You will become involved in ministries in your community, and you will make a difference.

Since the inception of this vital program in 1976, more than 95,000 people have participated in it. EfM groups meet regionally in nearly every diocese of The Episcopal Church, in six provinces of the Anglican Communion, and in virtual classrooms with participants from across the globe. We would love to have you join us!

For complete details, visit efm.sewanee.edu.